More...
Modern English
for conversation

■ Karen A. Stafford

UNIVERSITY EDUCATION PRESS

Introduction

This book is the second in the **Modern English for Conversation** series, created specifically for low to intermediate level ESL college students. It is intended to be used as a regular text (covering 30 90-minute classroom sessions) but may also be used effectively as supplementary activity in the ESL classroom.

Modern English for Conversation introduces commonly-used American English expressions in suggested models for conversation, and students will be encouraged to personalize conversations and exercises using their own information. Pair work and discussion exercises will have students build their skills in formulating basic questions and answers, as well as eliciting opinions from partners or others in their groups The ESL instructor can enhance each lesson with guided discussions using the topics in the lesson, to review the lesson and its grammar/vocabulary if necessary. Colloquial expressions and pronunciation drills are introduced throughout to build and strengthen students' conversational skills, pronunciation and vocabulary.

Components
Conversations
Students will practice conversation models utilizing given examples which will introduce new vocabulary and commonly-used expressions. In some conversations, students may substitute their own ideas to converse, using situations which are natural to them.

Grammar
Basic grammar, mostly patterns already familiar to the students, will be introduced throughout the book and combined with new expressions to reinforce proper usage of those patterns.

Writing
A minimal amount of writing will be asked of the students- to fill in questionnaires and make their own sentences to offer their opinions. The writing will act as useful information exchange for the conversations and discussion in the lesson.

Pronunciation
Pronunciation and intonation will be stressed in drills and lessons throughout the book.

Group Discussion
Lessons requiring group discussion will bring students together to exchange and present their ideas, offering students the chance to state their own opinions and get information from others.

It is up to the instructor to decide the number of students per group in order to make the lesson most valuable and easily understood to that particular level of students.

Games
Interactive games are included to promote free conversation on a wide range of topics suitable for college-age students. The students will be able to go at their own pace in their groups with minimal guidance from the instructor.

Contents

Introductions…page 1
Self-introductions and simple Q & A partner activity, plus using superlative adjectives to talk about one's hometown.

Classroom expressions…page 2
Commonly-used classroom expressions and extra activity.

Human Bingo…page 3
Interactive Bingo game, students go around the classroom to get "yes" answers in order to get 5 in a row and win.

Holidays, months and ordinal numbers…page 4
Discussing holidays, the months in which they fall and a holiday questionnaire.

Categories game…pages 5, 6, 7
Vocabulary-boosting game. Dictionaries recommended for this exercise.

Clothes and accessories…pages 8, 9
Singular & plural clothing/accessory items.

Clothes and accessories…page 10
Vocabulary and conversation introducing colors, patterns and prices.

Shopping and prices…page 11
Vocabulary and conversation with clothing sizes and materials.

Giving compliments…page 12
Basic expressions and simple conversation practice.

I've never done it…page 13
Using past-tense and the past participle.

Times & past-tense verbs…page 14
Students discuss their routines and what time they did various things.

Abbreviations…pages 15, 16, 17
Group work asking and answering questions about common abbreviations.

How often…?...page 19
Pair work with adverbs of frequency.

How often…?...page 20
Questionnaire and pair practice.

Word usage…How…page 21
Answering questions using the information question word 'how' + pair work.

What do you bring on your travels?...page 22
Travel questionnaire introducing new vocabulary, and group work.

The "Threes" Conversation Game…page 23
Board game for groups. (*Bring dice to class for this activity.)

What's the difference? Part One…page 25
Studying the difference between *interesting*, *funny* and *fun*.

Categories....page 26
Making categories using fruit and vegetable pages in back of book.

Comparative adjectives...page 27
Learning comparative adjectives.

Comparative adjectives (part II)...page 28
Questionnaire with pair work.

What's the difference?...page 29
How to explain the differences between two similar things.

Activities...page 30
Planning activities using original ideas (vocabulary).

Homophones *part one*...**page 31**
Using homophones in conversations.

Giving directions...page 32
Giving directions/instructions using frequency markers. Students will also get a chance to show their illustration skills.

Making a questionnaire...pages 33, 34
In groups, students will practice with the given questionnaire, then create one of their own. Students will practice formulating yes/no questions as well as information questions.

Pronunciation and spelling...pages 35, 37, 38
Pronunciation practice (dividing words into syllables), and asking/answering questions with picture cards.

What do they have in common?...page 39
Finding what groups of word have in common. Can be done in pairs or groups.

Reading large numbers-Part One...page 40
Reading dates, talking about personal historical events, asking questions.

Reading large numbers-Part Two...page 41
Reading numbers 5-digits and larger, and using them as prices in conversations.

Games Page...page 42
Vocabulary-building games. Can be done in pairs or small groups.

Getting sick...and getting better!...page 43
Discussing common ailments in conversations. Medical terminology pronunciation practice.

Countable and uncountable nouns...page 44
Learning the "rules" to distinguish countable/uncountable nouns, & a questionnaire.

I've never done it...page 45
This is a good exercise to get students to think, and also stresses formulating grammatically-correct sentences using the past-participle.

What are you afraid of?...page 46

Questionnaire and discussion, good for pair work.

Likes and dislikes...page 47

Students discuss their likes and dislikes.

What do you have in common?...page 48

Students ask questions to find out what they have in common with their partner.

Verbs- past tense and past participle...page 49

Students practice asking/making questions with the past-participle. Have them refer to the verb list in the back of the book.

What's the difference? Part Two...page 50

Studying the difference between *say, tell* and *talk*.

The Conversation Game...page 51

Board game for groups. (*Bring dice to class for this activity.)

Countries and nationalities...page 53

Learning countries/nationalities and what items are produced around the world.

Describing things...page 54

Describing animals, clothing, people and places.

Travel plans...page 55

Travel conversations, pair work.

Homophones *part two*...page 56

Using homophones in conversations.

Opposites Board game...page 57

Board game for groups. (*Bring dice to class for this activity.)

Usage- when and when not to use "to"...page 59

The word "to" is frequently misused by ESL speakers, this lesson will clarify its usage. Conversation practice for pair work.

Trivia Game...page 60

Group activity. Answers (for MC only!) given in back of book.

Present perfect tense with *Already & Yet*...page 61

Students will ask and answer questions with the expressions 'already' and 'yet'.

Fruit and Vegetable Crossword...page 62

Students can use fruit and vegetable pages in back of book to help with spelling.

Word usage- *With*...page 63

Introduces usage of the preposition 'with'. Conversation practice for pairs.

Compound words...page 64

Making compound words.

When was the last time you... ...page 65

Discussing the past.

Analogies...page 66

This lesson can be done as pair work or in groups. Students decide what words fit in the charts, then make up some of their own.

Blood types...page 67

Students see if the blood type character description is accurate for their own characters. (Refer to glossary in back of book for help with difficult vocabulary)

How "eco-friendly" are you?...page 68

Introduces the expressions reduce, reuse and recycle. Vocabulary-building activity and questionnaire.

Vocabulary Review Crossword...page 69

Crossword contains vocabulary introduced throughout the book.

Fruits and vegetables pages...pages 70, 71, 72

Illustrated pages for reference.

Verb list...page 73

List of infinitive/ past tense / past participle verbs for reference.

Trivia game questions...pages 74, 75

To be used for Trivia Game on page 60. This page should only be viewed by the MC during the game.

Answer key...page76

Answer keys to **Reading large numbers, Abbreviations,** and crosswords.

Category page...page 77

Extra page, should groups want to do this again.

English-Japanese glossary...pages 78, 79

Introductions

Hi! I'm_____ _____(name- first/last)
I live in _____(town). It's near_____.
My favorite things are _____ & _____.
Some things I don't like are_____, _____
or_____.

Getting personal information. Answer the questions, then ask your partner.

	Me	**Partner**
1. What is your favorite color?	_____	_____
2. What is a dream you have?	_____	_____
3. How many TVs do you have?	_____	_____
4. What animals do you like?	_____	_____
5. What do you want to buy now?	_____	_____
6. What is your favorite season?	_____	_____
7. What sports do you like?	_____	_____
8. What are 3 things you have in your bag?	_____	_____
9. What did you eat last night?	_____	_____
10. Where did you go, on your last trip?	_____	_____

Talking about your hometowns (using superlative adjectives)
1. The most famous food is_____.
2. The tallest building is_____.
3. The best place for shopping is_____.
4. The most popular tourist spot is _____.
5. The most beautiful nature spot is_____.
6. The worst weather is in_____(month).
7. The most delicious thing to eat is_____.

Now, make some sentences of your own!

1._____

2._____

3._____

Hints: the most exciting festival, the nicest park, the oldest building, the best season, the best restaurant, the oldest university, the most expensive food, the most popular temple, the biggest factory, etc.

Classroom expressions

Learn them, know them, use them!!!

Can you repeat that?
Sorry?

What's the date?

Can I borrow your (pen/ eraser/ ruler)?

How do you spell_____?
How do you spell that?

I can't pronounce it.
How do you pronounce that?

What's your first name?
         last name?

What does_____mean?
(It means_____.)

What's (*nasubi*) in English?
What's that in English?
How do you say (*nasubi*) in English?

May I use the restroom?
May I be excused?

She's/ he's absent.

Long time no see!

See you next week.
See you!

Have a nice weekend!
Have a nice holiday!

Activity: Conversation practice
A) Can I borrow your_____?
B) Sure, here.

Activity: Practice with gestures!

A) May I use the restroom?
B) Sure, go ahead.

A) May I be excused?
B) What's wrong?

A) _____.
B) Oh, OK.

Activity: Make 3 cards.
Card 1: Draw a picture of something your partner doesn't know in English.
Card 2: Draw a picture of any item.
Card 3: Write a very difficult word.
Practice:

A) What's that in English?
B) _____.

A) How do you spell that?
B) _____.

A) How do you pronounce that?
B) _____.

Human Bingo

Go around the room and ask people the questions. If they answer "yes", circle the question and write their name below it. If they answer "no", ask another person.
If you get 5 in a row, shout "Bingo!"

Did you eat fruit today?	Do you like to play games on your computer?	Does your family have a two-story house?	Do you like dogs?	Have you used the train in the past 2 weeks?
Do you like raw fish?	Have you ever been to a World Heritage Site?	Can you say "Thank you" in 3 languages?	Did you go shopping last weekend?	Do you wear pink?
Did you do the laundry this week?	Do you have more than 7 T-shirts?	Do you have an expensive wallet?	Can you whistle?	Have you ever slept in a tent?
Can you drive a car?	Have you ever killed a cockroach?	Can you do a handstand?	Do you bake?	Did your cell phone cost over ¥30,000?
Do you like to watch the news?	Did you buy a drink in a PET bottle last week?	Have you ever been to Disneyland?	Can you make a paper airplane?	Do you read magazines?

Holidays, months and ordinal numbers

Write the holidays/ special days under the months.

Culture Day	Christmas Day	Children's Day	Respect for the Aged Day
Sports Day	New Year's Eve	Valentine's Day	Showa Day
Christmas Eve	Outdoor Hot Spring Day	Halloween	Mother's Day
Emperor's birthday	Spring Equinox Day	New Year's Day	Coming of Age Day
Father's Day	National Founding Day	Sea Day	Labor Day

January

_____
_____
_____
_____

February

_____
_____
_____
_____

March

_____
_____
_____
_____

April

_____
_____
_____
_____

May

_____
_____
_____
_____

June

_____
_____
_____
_____

July

_____
_____
_____
_____

August

_____
_____
_____
_____

September

_____
_____
_____
_____

October

_____
_____
_____
_____

November

_____
_____
_____
_____

December

_____
_____
_____
_____

Now, practice this conversation with other students to get the exact dates! (Use a calendar!)

A) When's **Mother's Day**?
B) It's **May 10th.**

Now, find out the birthdays of some students. Write them on the lines below.

"When's your birthday?"

_____'s birthday is _____ ____.
_____'s birthday is _____ ____.
_____'s birthday is _____ ____.
_____'s birthday is _____ ____.

Mini-questionnaire:

1. What's your favorite holiday?_____
Why do you like it?_____
2. When is the next holiday?_____
What will you do on this day?_____

How to play the **Categories Game**-
Divide class into groups. Have each group think of a **5-letter word**. Write the letters of that word next to the word "category".
Cut out the category cards below. Groups choose 4 cards.
Write categories in the boxes (below "category") and make words beginning with the first letter on the spaces above pertaining to those categories.

Animals	Sports
Sweets	I have one now
We love it!	We hate it!
Things we do at school/work	Electronics / appliances
It's foreign…	Our favorite things…
Famous People	Occupations
About jewelry…	I can't do it…
Vegetables	Fruits
Holidays & Special days	It's *very very* expensive!
Words with double letters	About winter
About summer	White things

Category

Clothes & accessories- Part Two Plural items

Write the names of the items on the lines. The answers are in the word box.

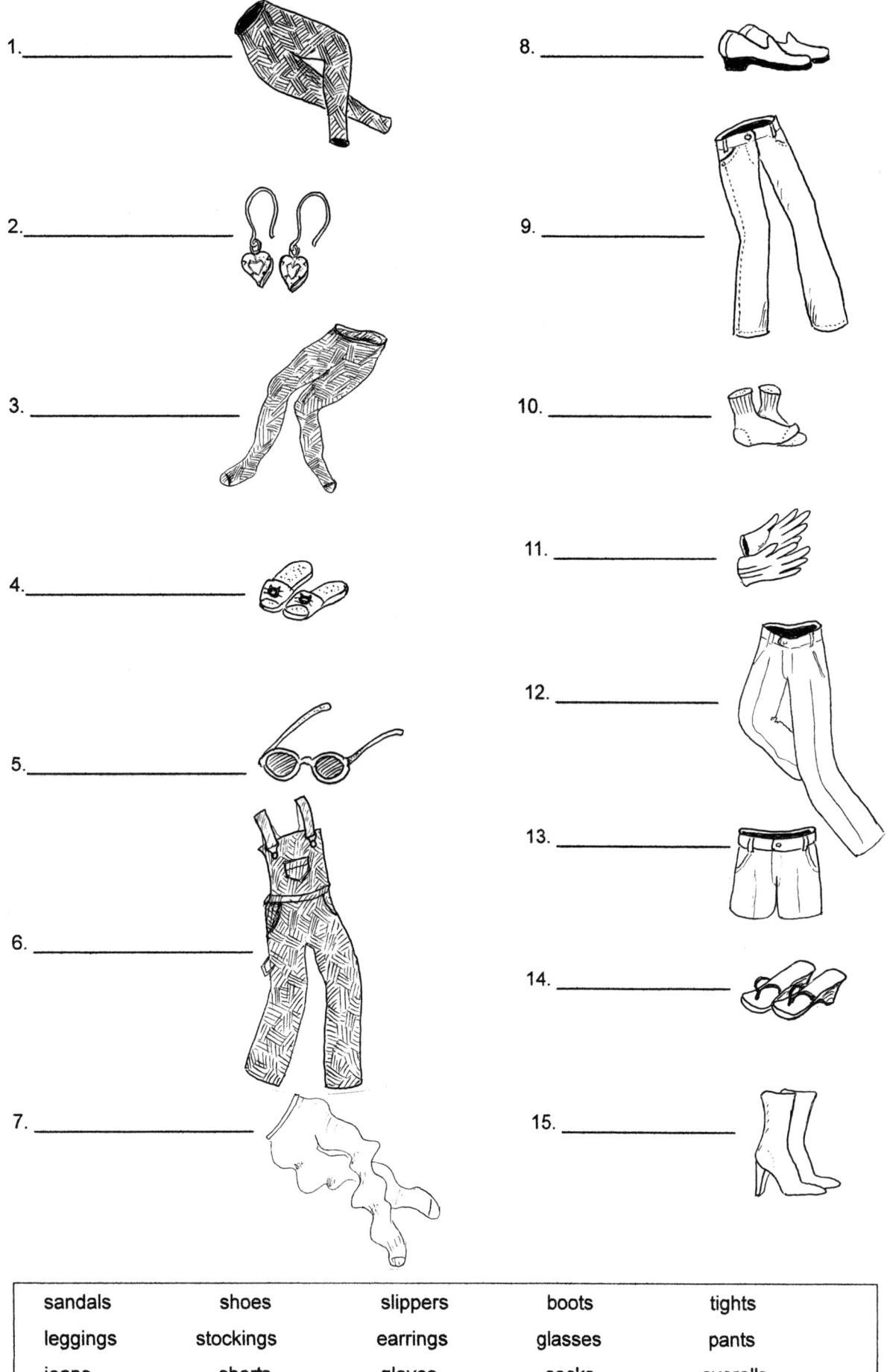

1. _____
2. _____
3. _____
4. _____
5. _____
6. _____
7. _____
8. _____
9. _____
10. _____
11. _____
12. _____
13. _____
14. _____
15. _____

sandals	shoes	slippers	boots	tights
leggings	stockings	earrings	glasses	pants
jeans	shorts	gloves	socks	overalls

Clothes & accessories- Part three Activity

Color the boxes

red ☐   orange ☐   yellow ☐   green ☐   light blue ☐

purple ☐   pink ☐   white ☐   beige ☐   black ☐

brown ☐   white ☐   silver ☐   gray ☐   gold ☐

Learn these patterns

striped   polka-dot   leopard print   paisley

camouflage

First, color some of the items on the clothes/accessories pages.
Next, write some *realistic* prices next to the items.
Then, practice the conversations below.

Situation: you are shopping at a mall. (use items from the *singular* page!)

You) Excuse me, how much is this_____ _____?
Clerk) It's _____.
You) Oh, I can't afford that...
Clerk) But it's 50% off this week, so it's only_____!
You) Great! I'll take it!

plaid

(Now, use items from the *plurals* page!)
You) May I see those_____ _____?
Clerk) Certainly. Here you are.
You) Wow, they're really nice!
Clerk) ...and they're on sale today! They're only_____!
You) Great! I'll take them!

zebra striped

Game; "Who is it?" Write hints about what one person is wearing. Class, try to guess who it is.

Example: This person has a blue T-shirt, a silver watch, black pants and white sneakers.

— 10 —

Shopping and Prices

Shoe Sizes in the US/Japan

US	Japan
5	22
5 1/2	22.5
6	23
6 1/2	23.5
7	24
7 1/2	24.5
8	25
8 1/2	25.5
9	26
9 1/2	26.5

Questionnaire   **Me**   **Partner**

1. What's your shoe size? _____ _____
2. What's your favorite color? _____ _____
3. What's your shirt size? _____ _____
4. What words best describe your taste in clothes?

Me:_____

Partner:_____

Shopping conversations

Singular

A) I bought a_____ _____(when).
B) Oh, how much was it?
A) It was _____yen.
B) Was it on sale?
A) No, that was the regular price. / Yes, the regular price was _____yen.

Draw it!

Plural

A) I bought some _____ _____(when).
B) Oh, how much **were they**?
A) **They were**_____yen.
B) **Were they** on sale?
A) No, that was the regular price. / Yes, the regular price was_____yen.

Draw them!

What are you wearing today? Ex. I'm wearing a purple blouse. I'm wearing brown boots.

1._____

2._____

3._____

What is it made of? Ex. My blouse is made of cotton. My boots are made of vinyl.

1._____

2._____

3._____

polyester   nylon   silk   acrylic   wool   leather   silk   rayon   linen

Giving compliments

Point 1- Mentioning the item

"That's a nice { skirt!" / dress!" / necklace!" }

"Those are nice { earrings!" / sunglasses!" / boots!" }

"I like your { sweater!" / blouse!" / hat!" }

"That { skirt / dress / scarf } looks good on you!"

Point 2- Getting more information

a. Where's it from?*
b. What's it made of?**
c. It looks expensive/heavy, etc.

*
> My father gave it to me.
> I got it as a wedding present.
> I bought it in Switzerland.
> It was a souvenir from my friend who went to Italy.
> I bought it at Tenmaya.
> I can't remember *where* I got it.

Sample Conversations

A) Nice tie, Bob!
B) Oh thanks. I got it at Disneyland!

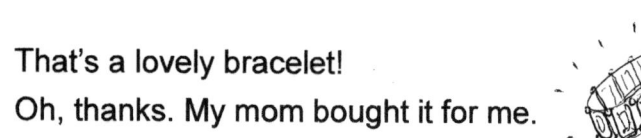

A) That's a lovely bracelet!
B) Oh, thanks. My mom bought it for me.
A) What's it made of?
B) It's silver.
A) And what are those stones?
B) I'm not sure. Blue topaz, I think...

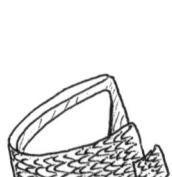

**
> gold
> silver
> platinum
> stainless steel
> titanium
> leather
> vinyl
> plastic
> polyester
> acrylic
> rayon
> cotton
> linen
> silk
> wool
> denim

A) Wow! What's that?
B) It's my new wallet. Like it?
A) Yeah, it's really neat! What is it, alligator?
B) No, it's lizard skin.
A) Lizard skin?! I've never seen a lizard skin wallet before!

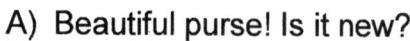

A) Beautiful purse! Is it new?
B) Yeah, I bought it last weekend.
A) It looks expensive...
B) It *was*. It cost ¥80,000! I used my bonus...

I've Never Done It

What are some things that **many people your age** have done, but you haven't.

For example:
I've never been to Tokyo Disneyland.
I've never read a Harry Potter book.
I've never eaten a Big Mac.
I've never had a flu shot.

1. _____

2. _____

3. _____

4. _____

5. _____

Listen to your partner's sentences. Which one surprised you most?

He's/ she's never_____

Can you make some guesses about some things your partner has **probably** never done? Are you right or wrong? (Ask "Have you ever…?)

For example:
I think she's never been fishing.
I think she's never drunk French champagne.
I think she's never spent over ¥50,000 on a purse.   right   wrong

1. _____ _____ _____

2. _____ _____ _____

3. _____ _____ _____

4. _____ _____ _____

Times & past-tense verbs

Answer the questions in complete sentences, using past-tense verbs. Use the word list in the back of the book to help you. Ask your partner the questions, and write your partner's answers, too.

Partner

1. What time did you get up this morning?
   I _____ at _____.   _____
2. What time did you get here today?
   I _____ at _____.   _____
3. What time did you eat dinner last night?
   I _____ at _____.   _____
4. What time did you take a bath/shower yesterday?
   I _____ at _____.   _____
5. What time did you go to bed last night?
   I _____ at _____.   _____
6. What time did you get up on Sunday?
   I _____ at _____.   _____

What did you do *yesterday*? Look at the timeline, and write what you did at those times. Then, ask your partner *"What did you do at 9:15?"* etc.

4:30am _____

6:00am _____

7:45am _____

9:15am _____

Noon (12:00) _____

3:30pm _____

6:00pm _____

9:15pm _____

11:00pm _____

1:00am _____

Abbreviations Group work

Cut out the abbreviations cards on the next page, and then practice the conversation.

A) What does _____ mean?
B) It means _____.

Are there any other abbreviations you know? Work with your group, and write them below. Use a dictionary if you need to.

Abbreviation	Meaning
_____	_____
_____	_____
_____	_____
_____	_____
_____	_____
_____	_____
_____	_____
_____	_____
_____	_____
_____	_____

Does he have **SARS**?
No, it looks like **BSE**...
Is she the **AD**?
No, she's the **DA**!
PM me **ASAP**!
Hurry! Get the **AED**!
It's OK, I know **CPR**
Whose **PET** bottle is this?

Abbreviation cards (cut out)

BSE	NPO	NEET	UK	GM
BMW	BYOB	ETC	NGO	MTV
NYPD	CNN	FIFA	MRI	PM
NG	PTA	MSG	4WD	JAF
KIX	UFO	UNESCO	USA	JR
VIP	TGIF	DIY	FBI	JAL

General Motors or Genetically Modified Food	United Kingdom (England, Scotland, Wales, & Northern Ireland)	Not Employed, in Education or Training	Non-Profit Organization	Bovine Spongiform Encephalopathy
Music Television	Non-Governmental Organization	Electronic Toll Collection	Bring Your Own Bottle	Bavarian Motor Works
Prime Minister or Private Message	Magnetic Resonance Imaging	Federation of International Football Association	Cable Network News	New York Police Department
Japan Automobile Federation	Four Wheel Drive	Monosodium Glutamate	Parent / Teacher's Association	No Good
Japan Railways	United States of America	United Nations Educational, Scientific and Cultural Organization	Unidentified Flying Object	Kansai International Airport
Japan Airlines	Federal Bureau of Investigation	Do It Yourself	Thank Goodness It's Friday	Very Important Person

How often...? Using adverbs of frequency

Read the adverbs:

always   often   sometimes   occasionally   hardly ever   never

With your partner, ask and answer questions using this conversation:

A) How often do you_____?
B) I ___(adverb)___ _____.

1. ride the train
2. eat chocolate
3. cook
4. clean your room
5. sleep in class/at work
6. go to the bank/use an ATM
7. get sick (catch a cold, etc)
8. use a computer
9. play with animals
10. wear a hat
11. complain about _____
12. get souvenirs
13. read books
14. spill your drink

Next, choose **one** of the topics below, and write true sentences about YOU.

school   sports   shopping   food   animals   friends

1. I always_____.

2. I often _____.

3. I sometimes _____.

4. I occasionally _____.

5. I hardly ever _____.

6. I never _____.

Now, ask your partner questions using the **verbs** from the above exercise.
For example: A) Do you ever <u>play tennis on the weekend?</u>
            B) Yes, sometimes.

            A) Do you ever <u>watch baseball on TV?</u>
            B) No, never.

— 19 —

How often?

Fill in the questionnaire about yourself, then practice conversations with your partner.

Fill in the blanks. Use **simple verbs** in your answers.

1. Something I do every day_____
   (   )
2. Something I hate to do_____
   (   )
3. Something I can't do well_____
   (   )
4. Something I do at school(or at work)_____
   (   )
5. Something I want to do all the time, but can't_____
   (   )
6. Something I love to do_____
   (   )
7. Something I spend a lot of money to do_____
   (   )
8. Something I do that I don't mind*_____
   (   )

(*Most people don't really like doing this.)

Study this expression table:

once a		**week**
twice a	⇨	**month**
three times		**year**
four times a		
etc.		

But......Once in two month**s**. / Once in three month**s**. Etc.
or "I never..."

Now, look at your partner's information and ask questions. You will write your answers in the parentheses.
Example:
You) How often do you <u>ride a bicycle?</u>
Partner) I <u>ride a bicycle</u> <u>twice a week.</u>   **or**   I <u>never</u> <u>ride a bicycle.</u>

Word usage- *How*

How can be used to ask **manner/meaning/extent/reason and condition.**

~do you eat this?	~old are you?
~much does it weigh?	~high is it?
~do you pronounce that?	~much do you want?

Use the expressions above in the blanks

1. How_____?
2. How_____?
3. How_____?
4. How_____?
5. How_____?
6. How_____?

Ask your partner the questions-
1. How do you spell your name?
2. How many people are there in your family?
3. How do you usually get here?
4. How is your mother/ father?
5. How heavy is your bag/ purse?
6. How much cash/ how many coins do you have today?

Questionnaire- Write your answers, then get your partner's answers.

	me	partner
1. How much TV do you watch? (hours/day)	_____	_____
2. How tall are you?	_____	_____
3. How often do you eat meat?	_____	_____
4. How do you sing?	_____	_____
5. How will you spend the next holiday?	_____	_____
6. How many books do you have?	_____	_____
7. How long do you usually sleep?	_____	_____
8. How many cookies can you eat?	_____	_____

What do you bring on your travels?

Circle the items you usually bring with you.

a map	snacks	stomach medicine
a guidebook	gum	a toothbrush & toothpaste
a credit card	comfortable shoes	a comb or brush
cash (money)	tissues	a flashlight
a passport	aspirin	a memo pad
a folding umbrella	ear plugs	a hat
a cell phone	sunscreen	a camera

What other things do you usually bring?

_____   _____   _____
_____   _____   _____

What are some things you **never** bring?

_____   _____   _____
_____   _____   _____

Now, ask other people if they bring these things. Check it "✓" if they say "yes", put an "X" if they say "no".

Now, report the answers.

All of us bring_____, _____ and _____.

Some of us bring_____, _____ and_____.

One of us brings_____.

None of us bring_____ or _____.

How about your last trip? Where did you go? What did you bring?

I went to_____ for _____(how long)
I brought_____
_____.

Now, ask your partner questions.
Example: "Why did you bring a credit card?"   "Because I wanted to go shopping."
         "Why did you bring hiking boots?"   "Because I went to climb Mt. Fuji."

❖ The "Threes" Conversation Game ❖

Roll the die and read what it says on the space.
Answer the question, and partners, give a comment!

START

FINISH

- Name 3 foods you would like to eat tonight
- What are 3 things you always say?
- Name 3 things you don't need.
- What are 3 things you planned to do last year, but didn't do?
- Name 3 things you heard in the news.
- Name 3 things you have in your refrigerator now.
- Name 3 stinky things.
- Roll again!
- Name 3 countries where the people speak English.
- Who are 3 people you would like to have dinner with? (living or dead)
- Name 3 stupid things that people do.
- Name 3 cities you have visited, and what you did there.
- Name your 3 favorite toppings for pizza.
- Name 3 things that are very popular now.
- Name your 3 best qualities.
- Roll again!
- Name your 3 favorite toppings for sushi.
- What are 3 things you've never tried?
- What are 3 things you've always wanted to do?
- Name 3 very, very cute animals.
- Tell us 3 things you always carry with you
- Name 3 things you do before you leave the house.

— 23 —

What's the difference? Part One

Notice the differences in the meanings of these words:
interesting (adj.)- something that holds your interest.
funny (adj.)- something that amuses you, and usually makes you laugh.
fun (adj. & noun)- something that gives you amusement or enjoyment.

Fill in the blanks with the correct words.

Mom) How was your day?
Son) Oh, pretty_____. We had a field trip to a dairy farm.
Mom) What did you do there?
Son) We learned how to milk a cow!
Mom) Wow, that sounds_____!
Son) Actually, the cow kicked our teacher! It was so_____,
    We couldn't stop laughing!

Girl) Let's do something _____ this weekend!
Boy) Sounds good! How about going to sing karaoke?
Girl) No, something *more*_____ than that!
Boy) I got it! We can go ride that new rollercoaster!
Girl) Now *that* sounds like _____!

Student A) Wow! That was a really _____ lecture!
    Professor Simpson really knows a lot about global warming!
Student B) _____? I didn't think so. I was bored stiff.
    But I had a really good nap...

Questionnaire   Write your answers, then ask your partner the questions.
1. What is something **interesting** that you have done?_____

2. What are some subjects(topics) that you find **interesting**?_____

3. What is something **fun** that you did recently?_____

4. What is something **funny** that you can do?_____

Categories-
With your partner, use the fruit & vegetable pages in the back of the book to fill in the category charts. Then, make some of your own.

You eat it in summer	**It grows in the ground**	**It's good in desserts**
_____	_____	_____
_____	_____	_____
_____	_____	_____
_____	_____	_____

You *can't* eat it raw	**We've never tried it**	**It's used in salads**
_____	_____	_____
_____	_____	_____
_____	_____	_____
_____	_____	_____

It's grown in my region	_____	_____
_____	_____	_____
_____	_____	_____
_____	_____	_____
_____	_____	_____

Comparative adjectives
Fill in the blanks

+ er
cold-colder
clean-cleaner
small-smaller
smart-smarter
tall-taller
short-shorter
long-longer
cheap-cheaper
fast-_____
slow-_____
young_____
old-_____
sweet_____

+ ier
busy-busier
silly-sillier
scary-scarier-
spicy-spicier
crazy-crazier
lazy-lazier
heavy-_____
pretty-_____
happy-_____
dirty-_____

irregulars
good-better
bad-worse
far-farther

double letters + er
hot-hotter
fat-fatter
wet-_____
thin-_____

more + _____
interesting-more interesting
beautiful-more beautiful
expensive-more expensive
popular-more popular
intelligent-more intelligent
dangerous-more dangerous
unusual-more unusual
comfortable-_____
famous-_____
difficult-_____
delicious-_____
crowded-_____

Now, fill in the blanks using words from the word box:

more useful	easier
higher	more populated
cheaper	worse
hotter	more comfortable
more exciting	more unusual

A banana is _____ than a peach.

A cell phone is _____ than a stapler.

A broken leg is _____ than a sprained wrist.

California is _____ than New York.

A menu is _____ to understand than a map.

Mt Kilimanjaro is _____ than Mt Fuji.

Sneakers are _____ than high heels.

Mexican food is _____ than Japanese food.

An amusement park is _____ than an aquarium.

An armadillo is a _____ pet than a rabbit.

Comparative adjectives (part II)
Questionnaire

Write your answers, then ask your partner the question, and put a check (✓) in the boxes.

	Me	Partner

1. What time did you get up this morning? _____ _____

I got up ☐ **earlier** / ☐ **later** than my partner.

2. How long does it take you to get ready in the morning? _____ _____

I am ☐ **faster** / ☐ **slower** than my partner.

3. How tall are you? _____ _____

I am ☐ **taller** / ☐ **shorter** than my partner.

4. How happy are you now? _____ _____

☐ I am happier than my partner.
☐ My partner is happier than I am.

5. How heavy is your bag (or purse)? _____ _____

My bag is ☐ **heavier** / ☐ **lighter** than my partner's bag.

6. How old is your pen/ pencil? _____ _____

My pen/ pencil is ☐ **older** / ☐ **newer** than my partner's.

7. How far from here do you live? _____ _____

I live ☐ **closer** / ☐ **farther** than my partner.

Now make some of your own questions. Be sure to *use adjectives!!!*

_____ _____ _____

_____

_____ _____ _____

_____

What's the difference?

There are several ways you can explain the difference(s) between two things. Read the examples:

What's the difference between a mountain and a hill?

You can explain using a **comparative adjective** in one sentence:

A mountain is higher than a hill.

Or you can explain using a **negative** in one sentence.

A mountain is high, but a hill is not so high./ but a hill is low.

Or you can use **two simple sentences.**

A mountain is high. A hill is low.

Got it? ☺

Now, see if you can explain the difference between these things-

What's the difference between…

1. A mug and a cup

_____

2. A hostel and a hotel

_____

3. Sake and wine

_____

4. Indian curry and Japanese curry

_____

5. A scooter and a motorcycle

_____

Can you make up a couple of your own? (When you finish, ask your partner)

1. _____ and _____

_____

2. _____ and _____

_____

Activities

Fill in the boxes with **items** you will need for each activity, and practice the conversations.

Going to the beach	Going to the mall	Going camping
_____	_____	_____
_____	_____	_____
_____	_____	_____

A) How about _____ today?
B) That's a good idea. If I bring _____,
   can you bring the _____?
A) No problem! Oh, and we definitely can't forget_____!

Some more activities....

Clean the house	Make a cake	Wash my car
_____	_____	_____
_____	_____	_____
_____	_____	_____

A) Can you help me _____ this afternoon?
B) Oh, OK. What do you want me to do?
A) I already have _____ and_____, but can you
   get some _____ from the supermarket?
B) Sure, no problem. Just give me the money!

Next, *you and your partner* plan an activity. Fill in the conversation below, and don't forget the items you will need!

A) Hi_____! (name)
   Do you want to_____on Sunday?
B) Oh, that sounds_____! (great /fun /good /exciting, etc.)
A) Well, we need to get some _____ first!
B) Yeah, and we can't forget the _____ or
   _____!

Homophones *part one*

Homophones are words that sound the same, but have different spelling and meaning. Read the words below, and use them in the conversations.

wear	pear	weigh	hour	flower	meet	right
where	pair	way	our	flour	meat	write

1. A) Hi! My name's Bill.
   B) Nice to _____ you, Bill. I'm Paul.

   C) What's for dinner?
   D) I can't decide- what do *you* want- _____ or fish?

2. A) Is this your new e-mail address?
   B) No, that's not _____.
   A) Oh, then can you _____ it here, please?

3. A) _____ are my car keys?
   B) They're over here.

   C) What will you _____ to the party tonight?
   D) Oh, I don't know…probably a suit…

4. A) Do you need anything? I'm going to the supermarket now.
   B) Yeah, can you get some _____? I'm going to make a cake later…

   C) What kind of _____ is that?
   D) I don't know- it looks like a tulip…

5. A) Excuse me, which _____ is the station?
   B) Oh, it's that _____, about 5 minutes. You can't miss it.

   C) How much do you _____?
   D) Sorry, that's a secret!

6. A) Can you take _____ picture?
   B) Sure! Smile!

   C) I'm starving! When's lunch?
   D) In an _____. You'll have to wait!

7. A) Do we have any fruit?
   B) Yeah, there's an apple and a _____ in the refrigerator.

   C) Did you buy anything at the mall today?
   D) Yeah, they were having a big sale, so I bought a _____ of shoes.

Giving Directions

Using the sequence markers *first, next, after that* and *finally*, Create sets of illustrated directions. Write the captions below.

How to get spending money

First, massage his shoulders.

Next, wash his car.

After that, get him his favorite drink.

Finally, collect the money!

How to have a great party

First, call some friends.

Next, get some party favors.

After that, get some food.

Finally, start the party!

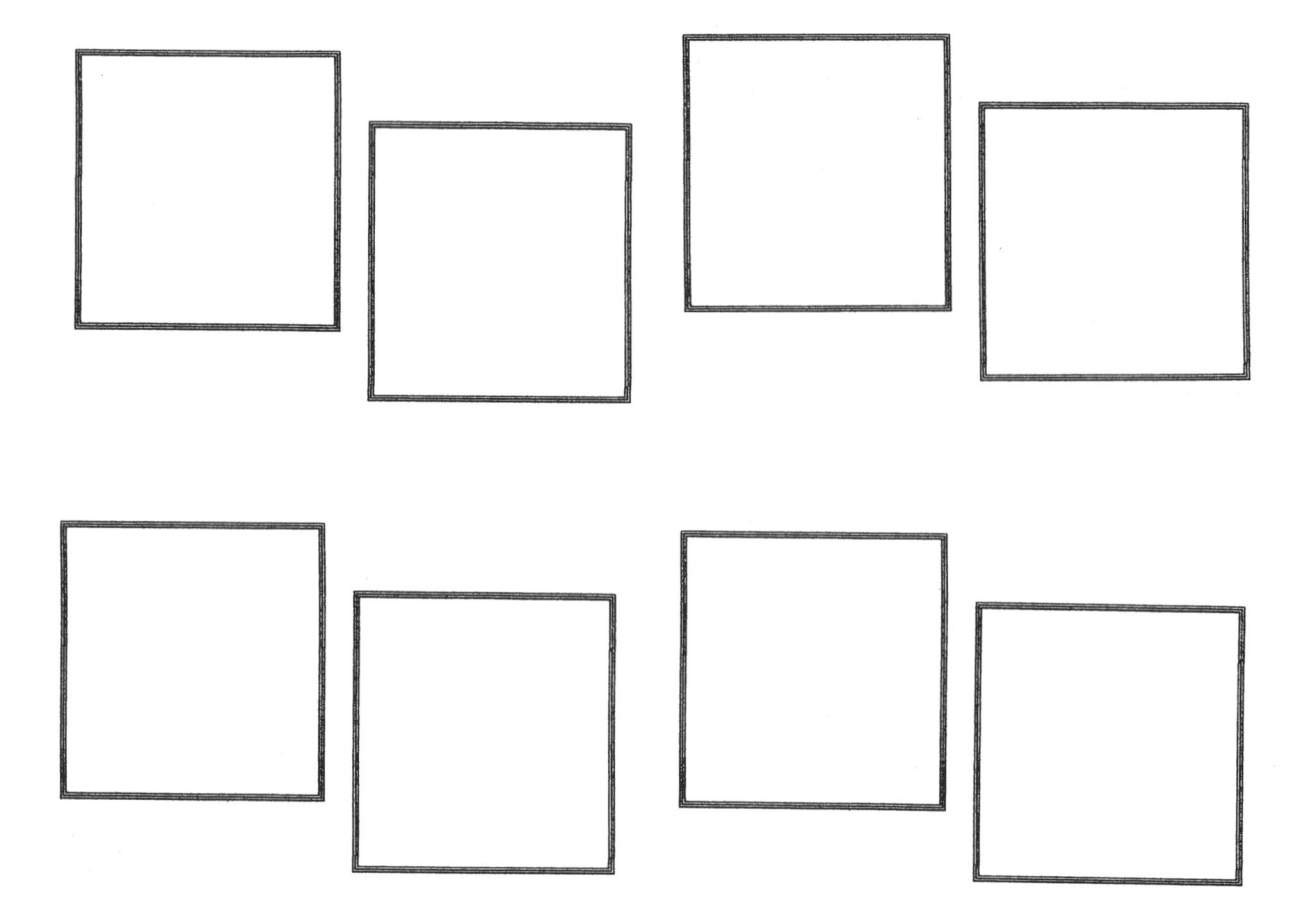

Making a questionnaire group work

Get into groups (3~4 people) and then decide your **topic**. Then, formulate 5 yes/no questions and 5 information questions. When you're finished, interview other people. The teacher will demonstrate using the questionnaire below.
(You can use the questionnaire format on the next page)

Topic: <u>Sweets</u> (✓ = yes, ✗ = no)

          a. b. c. d.

1. **Do you have a sweet tooth?** ☐ ☐ ☐ ☐

2. **Do you eat sweets every day?** ☐ ☐ ☐ ☐

3. **Do you spend more than ¥500 a week on sweets?** ☐ ☐ ☐ ☐

4. **When you eat at a restaurant, do you usually order dessert?** ☐ ☐ ☐ ☐

5. **Do you have more than 3 kinds of sweets at home now?** ☐ ☐ ☐ ☐

6. **What's your favorite sweet food?**
   a. _____ b. _____
   c. _____ d. _____

7. **When do you like to eat sweets?**
   a. _____ b. _____
   c. _____ d. _____

8. **If today was your birthday, what kind of cake would you like to eat?**
   a. _____ b. _____
   c. _____ d. _____

9. **What sweet food can you make?**
   a. _____ b. _____
   c. _____ d. _____

10. **What sweets do you usually carry with you?**
   a. _____ b. _____
   c. _____ d. _____

Making a questionnaire group work

Group members _____
_____

Topic: _____

(✓ = yes, ✗ = no)

a. b. c. d.

1. _____
   _____? ☐ ☐ ☐ ☐

2. _____
   _____? ☐ ☐ ☐ ☐

3. _____
   _____? ☐ ☐ ☐ ☐

4. _____
   _____? ☐ ☐ ☐ ☐

5. _____
   _____? ☐ ☐ ☐ ☐

6. _____ a. _____ b. _____
   _____? c. _____ d. _____

7. _____ a. _____ b. _____
   _____? c. _____ d. _____

8. _____ a. _____ b. _____
   _____? c. _____ d. _____

9. _____ a. _____ b. _____
   _____? c. _____ d. _____

10. _____ a. _____ b. _____
    _____? c. _____ d. _____

*Did you learn anything interesting from the results? What did you find out?

_____

Pronunciation and Spelling

How do you pronounce it? Divide the words with slashes for the syllables, and mark the accents.
Examples: stráw/ber/ry   a/na/cón/da   túr/tle

1. tomato
2. report
3. guitar

4. persimmon
5. eraser
6. influenza

7. mayonnaise
8. pizza
9. stadium

10. refrigerator
11. unicycle
12. pomegranate

13. mozzarella
14. cappuccino
15. McDonald`s

Conversation using word cards
Student A writes words(& #s) in spaces   ( )_____   ( )_____
                                             ( )_____   ( )_____
A) What's that in English?   ( )_____   ( )_____
B) "x x x".   ( )_____   ( )_____
A) How do you spell it?   ( )_____   ( )_____
B) "x-x-x".   ( )_____   ( )_____

What's that in English?

Practicing with plurals
Use things the students have, or things in the room.
(*If you don't know the English word, **ask the teacher!!!**)
Example:

A) What are those?
B) They're **curtains.**
A) How do you spell that?
B) **C-u-r-t-a-i-n-s.**

Write some new words you learned:

_____   _____

_____   _____

_____   _____

Notes:

Picture cards   Set A

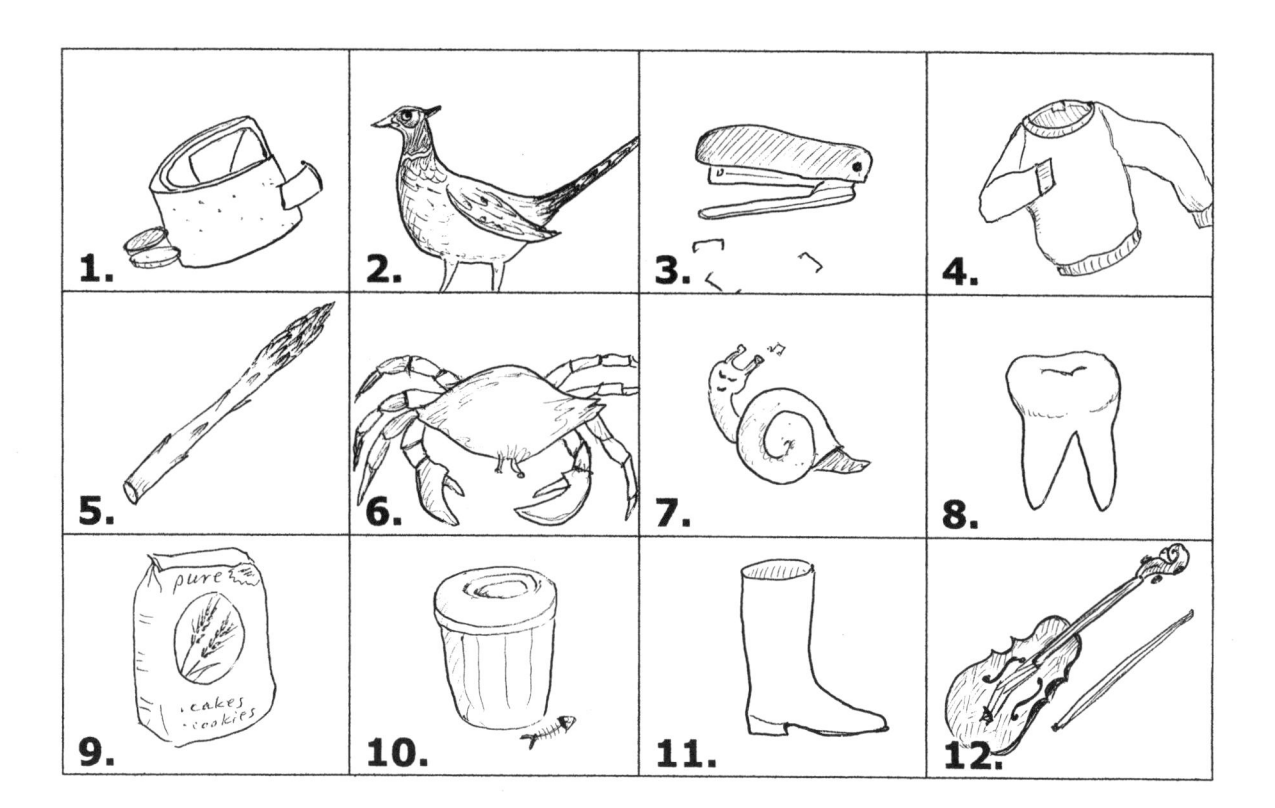

1.	2.	3.	4.
5.	6.	7.	8.
9.	10.	11.	12.

Picture cards   Set B

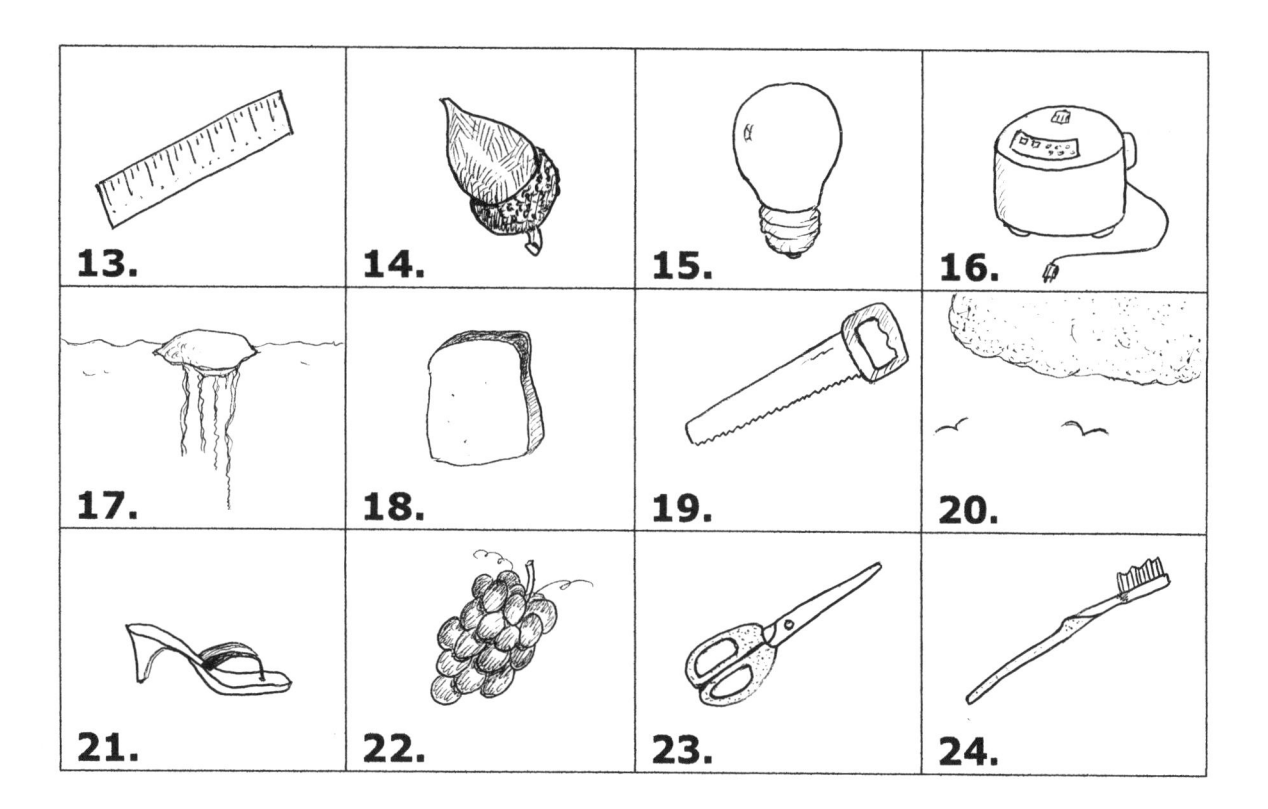

13.	14.	15.	16.
17.	18.	19.	20.
21.	22.	23.	24.

Word List A
1. wallet
2. pheasant
3. stapler
4. sweatshirt
5. asparagus
6. crab
7. snail
8. tooth
9. flour
10. garbage can
11. boot
12. violin

Word list B
13. ruler
14. acorn
15. light bulb
16. rice cooker
17. jellyfish
18. bread
19. saw
20. cloud
21. sandal
22. grapes
23. scissors
24. toothbrush

What do they have in common?
Study the word groups, and figure out what each group has in common.
Write the answer on the line below.
Example:

<u>tiger</u>   <u>dog</u>   <u>boar</u>   <u>snake</u>   <u>horse</u>
They are animals.   **or**   *They are signs of the Chinese zodiac.*

1. <u>cucumber</u>   <u>celery</u>   <u>lime</u>   <u>Muscat grapes</u>   <u>cabbage</u>
___

2. <u>cockroach</u>   <u>dragonfly</u>   <u>mosquito</u>   <u>centipede</u>   <u>cicada</u>
___

3. <u>comb</u>   <u>mirror</u>   <u>perfume</u>   <u>lipstick</u>   <u>handkerchief</u>
___

4. <u>toothbrush</u>   <u>toilet</u>   <u>cell phone</u>   <u>bed</u>   <u>shoes</u>
___

5. <u>refrigerator</u>   <u>plates</u>   <u>sink</u>   <u>forks</u>   <u>oven</u>
___

Now, write two of your own-

_____   _____   _____   _____   _____
_____

_____   _____   _____   _____   _____
_____

What do you have <u>in common</u> with your partner(s)?
(You might have to ask questions to find out!)

Example: <u>We are wearing watches.</u>   <u>We have a pet dog.</u>   <u>We don't like cold weather.</u>

1. _____

2. _____

3. _____

4. _____

Reading large numbers- Part One

Read dates (years) like this:

1492 fourteen ninety two

1776 seventeen seventy six

1995 nineteen ninety five

2000 two thousand

2007 two thousand seven

2010 two thousand ten/ twenty ten

Match exercise- take turns asking & answering the questions with your partner. See if you can guess the correct answer.

1. When did Neil Armstrong walk on the moon?
2. When did Hawaii become a part of the USA?
3. When was the Berlin Wall torn down?
4. When were the World Trade Center towers attacked?
5. When was the first powered airplane flight?
6. When did women in America get the right to vote?
7. When was the attack on Pearl Harbor?
8. When did Japan introduce a sales tax?
9. When did Martin Luther King Jr give his "I Have a Dream" speech?
10. When was the Great Hanshin Earthquake?

___a. in 1903.
___b. in 1995.
___c. in 1988.
___d. in 1941.
___e. in 1959.
___f. in 1963.
___g. in 2001.
___h. in 1969.
___i. in 1989.
___j. in 1920.

A history of YOU! What are some historical dates in your life? For example:

| I was born in… | I moved here in… | I met my best friend in … |
| I learned to_____in… | I got my driver's license in… | I had an accident in… |

Write them here…

_____
_____
_____
_____
_____

Now, think of some questions to ask your partner. See how many dates you can get! For example…

When did you get that scar?
When did you get those glasses/earrings/ jeans, etc.?
When did you travel abroad?
When did you start high school?

Reading large numbers- Part Two

Read numbers like this:

1000 one thousand
10,000 ten thousand
15,000 fifteen thousand
50,000 fifty thousand
100,000 one hundred thousand

150,000 one hundred fifty thousand
500,000 five hundred thousand
1,000,000 one million
10,000,000 ten million
1,000,000,000 one billion

Practice the conversations. Use the words/numbers on the right.

At an appliance store

You) May I see this rice cooker?

Clerk) Sure. It's a new model, we just got it today. It's only ¥28,000.

You) Oh, I don't have that much money! Do you have anything cheaper?

Clerk) This one over here is only ¥12,000...

You) It's perfect! I'll take it!

- Refrigerator
- ¥250,000
- ¥95,000

- Super-size plasma TV
- ¥970,000
- ¥300,000

- _____
- _____
- _____

With a friend

A) Look! I just bought some lottery tickets!
B) Oh, how much is the jackpot?
A) ¥10,000,000!
B) Have you ever won any money in the lottery?
A) Just once, but only ¥10,000...

- ¥200,000,000
- ¥1000

- ¥30,000,000
- ¥3000

At a real estate agency

A) I'm looking for homes in the Tokyo area.
B) We have some nice homes here, starting at ¥200,000,000...
A) Oh, that's much too expensive for me. How about in the suburbs?
B) Those start at around ¥50,000,000...
A) Hmm...Maybe you'd better show me some condominiums instead...

- Okayama
- ¥30,000,000
- ¥20,000,000

- Asahikawa
- ¥25,000,000
- ¥15,000,000

- _____
- _____
- _____

Games Page Try these short & easy games

English picture "shiri-tori" - Make new words beginning with the last letter of the picture.

[ ] ⇨ [ ] ⇨ [ ] ⇨ [ ] ⇨ [ ]
⇩
[ ] ⇦ [ ] ⇦ [ ] ⇦ [ ] ⇦ [ ]

How many words can you make?

How many words can you make from one word? For example:

BASKET ask, a, bet, bat, task, as, at, base, bask, etc.

How about from this word?

TEACHER

_____ _____ _____ _____
_____ _____ _____ _____
_____ _____ _____ _____
_____ _____ _____ _____
_____ _____ _____ _____

Find 10 things in the room that start with the letter "F".

_____ _____ _____ _____ _____
_____ _____ _____ _____ _____

Scavenger hunt: find these things in the room & write what you find!

- Something purple_____
- Something hot_____
- Something with the numbers 1,2 3_____
- Something you can eat_____
- A heart shape_____
- Something very heavy_____
- Something over 20 years old_____
- Something in a box_____
- Something sad_____
- Something new_____
- Something people don't like_____

Getting Sick...and getting better!

Match the *ailments* with the advice. Then, practice the exchanges.

____1. I have a sore throat.
____2. I have a stomachache.
____3. I have stiff shoulders.
____4. Ouch! I sprained my ankle!
____5. I feel dizzy.
____6. I have a runny nose.
____7. I have a backache.
____8. I have an earache.
____9. I think I might have hayfever.
____10. Oh no! I just cut my finger!

a. Get a massage!
b. Go to the ENT!
c. Get a band-aid!
d. Lie down!
e. Wear a mask!
f. Gargle!
g. Use a compress!
h. Take some stomach medicine!
i. Get some tissues!
j. Wrap it with a bandage!

What do **you** do? Write your answers.

What do you do if...
1. ...you're coming down with a cold? _____
2. ...you have a headache?_____
3. ...you have diarrhea?_____
4. ...you feel nauseous?_____

Practice the conversations using the above ailments and **what you do**. (Use gestures!)

A) What's wrong? You don't look so good.
B) I_____.
A) That's awful! You should_____.
B) Thanks, that's good advice. I'll do that.

Vocabulary (divide the syllables and mark the accent)

influenza
diabetes
obesity
stethoscope
osteoporosis
esophagus
antibiotics
thermometer

pediatrician
radiologist
nutritionist
gynecologist
ophthalmologist
pharmacist
cardiologist
urologist

Countable and uncountable nouns

Remember these basic rules for uncountable nouns-

Liquids and pastes- milk, water, gas, oil, juice, perfume, miso, mayonnaise, ketchup, soy sauce, detergent, etc.
Portions or shapes that change- cheese, fish, ice cream, money, meat, fish, tofu, etc.
Powder or small grains- sand, salt, detergent, pepper, sugar, rice, flour, etc.

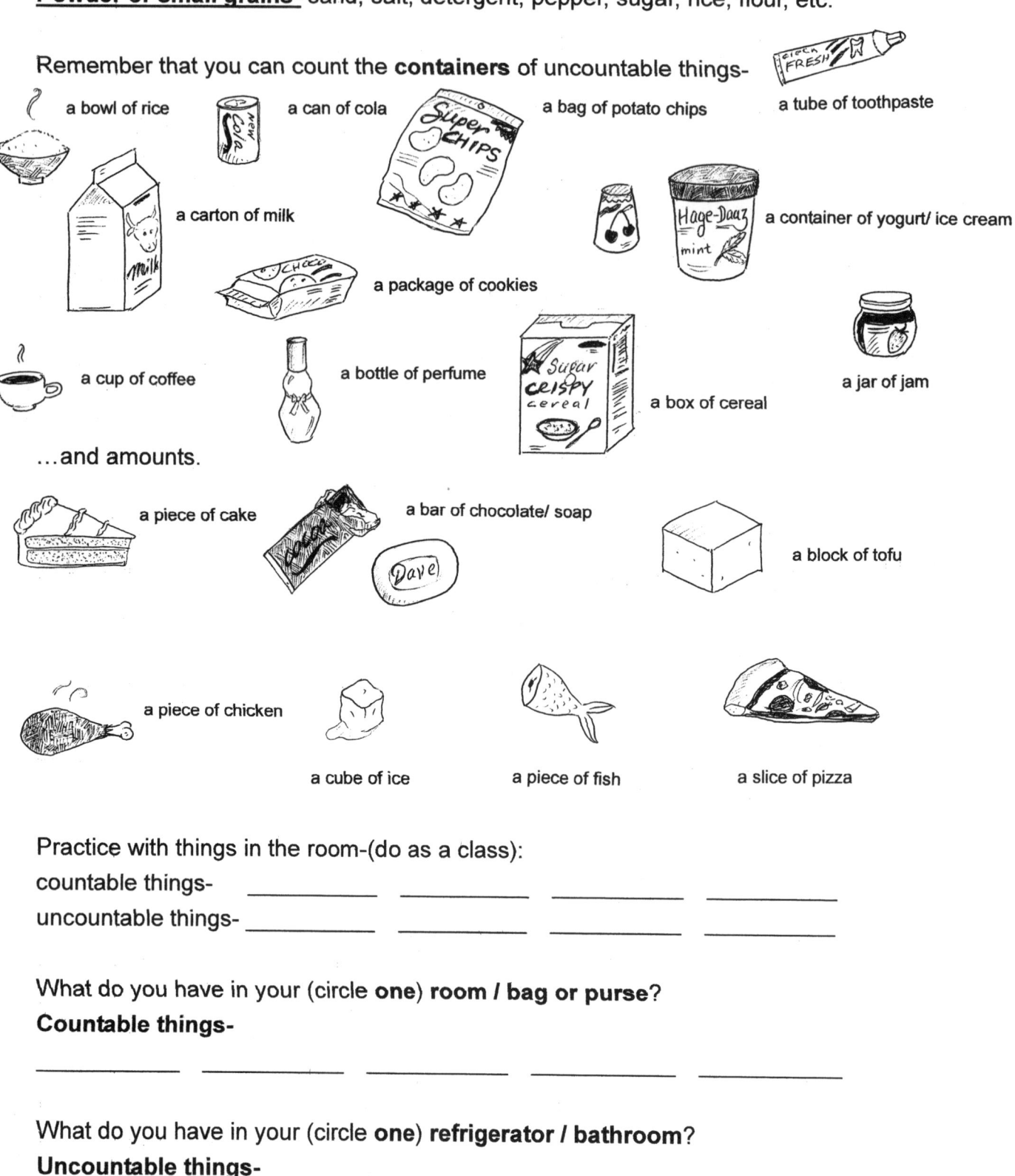

Remember that you can count the **containers** of uncountable things-

a bowl of rice   a can of cola   a bag of potato chips   a tube of toothpaste

a carton of milk

a package of cookies   a container of yogurt/ ice cream

a cup of coffee   a bottle of perfume   a box of cereal   a jar of jam

…and amounts.

a piece of cake   a bar of chocolate/ soap   a block of tofu

a piece of chicken   a cube of ice   a piece of fish   a slice of pizza

Practice with things in the room-(do as a class):
countable things-   _____ _____ _____ _____
uncountable things-   _____ _____ _____ _____

What do you have in your (circle **one**) **room / bag or purse**?
Countable things-

_____ _____ _____ _____ _____

What do you have in your (circle **one**) **refrigerator / bathroom**?
Uncountable things-

_____ _____ _____ _____ _____

I've never done it...(using past-participles)
What are some things that **many people your age** have done, but you haven't?

For example:

I've never been to Tokyo Disneyland.

I've never read a Harry Potter book.

I've never eaten a Big Mac.

I've never had a flu shot.

1. _____

2. _____

3. _____

4. _____

5. _____

Listen to your partner's sentences. Which one surprised you most?

He's/ she's never_____

Can you make some guesses about some things your partner has **probably** never done? Are you right or wrong? (Ask "Have you ever...?)

For example:

I think she's never been fishing.

I think she's never drunk French champagne.

I think she's never spent over ¥50,000 on a purse.   **right**   **wrong**

1. _____   _____   _____

2. _____   _____   _____

3. _____   _____   _____

4. _____   _____   _____

What are you afraid of?

People fear many things- some more than others. Name some common fears people have.

_____	_____	_____
_____	_____	_____
_____	_____	_____
_____	_____	

Which of the above do you fear the most?

_____

Which things did you fear when you were younger, but no longer fear?

_____

What are some things that are feared in your culture that are not feared in other cultures (and vice-versa)?_____

_____

Giving Advice- What would you advise your partner to do, to avoid his/her fears?

Use these expressions- **If I were you, I'd...   Why don't you...?   You should/shouldn't...**

Example: A) I'm afraid of deep water!   A) I'm afraid of aging!
B) Why don't you stay near the beach?   B) You should take vitamin supplements.

My fears	**Advice from my partner**	**Good advice? (yes/no)**
_____	_____	_____
_____	_____	_____
_____	_____	_____

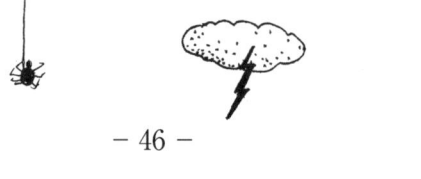

Likes and dislikes

Put the items/activities in the appropriate boxes. First, read the list with your teacher.

I love it

I like it

I don't like it

I hate it

- fishing
- winter
- going to museums
- doing housework
- traveling by train
- shopping for clothes
- spicy food
- swimming
- going to zoos
- thunder & lightning
- eating chocolate
- grocery shopping
- going to the dentist
- eating outside
- watching movies
- seafood
- getting up early
- baking
- going to hot springs
- fruit
- spring
- using the internet
- wearing a hat
- going to amusement parks
- staying up all night

Now, ask your partner: A) Do you like _____?
  B) Yes. I love it. / No, I don't like it.

Group work: choose one of the topics below & write 4 sentences.

outdoors   animals   work   entertainment   shopping   weather

We love_____.
We like_____.
We don't like_____.
We hate_____.

What do you have in common?

Asking questions to see what you & your partner have in common.

You will ask your partner some **yes/no questions**.
Here are some examples:

Do you like tomatoes? / ~wear shorts in the summer? / ~have a pet?
Are you a Pisces? / ~hungry now? / ~going to watch TV tonight?
Can you whistle? / ~hold a frog? / ~sing an English song?
Will you buy a car soon? / ~eat meat tonight? / ~go shopping tomorrow?

Next, write your questions below: **Things in common**

_____ me:____ a.____ b.____

_____ me:____ a.____ b.____

_____ me:____ a.____ b.____

_____ me:____ a.____ b.____

_____ me:____ a.____ b.____

_____ me:____ a.____ b.____

_____ me:____ a.____ b.____

Now, ask you partner the questions. Here are some examples:
You) Do you like summer?
Partner a) Yes I do.
You) Me, too!   (Then you put a ✓ in the spaces for things in common)

You) Do you like snakes?
Partner a) No, I don't.
You) Me neither.   (Then you put an **x** in the spaces)

You) Do you like big dogs?
Partner a) No, I don't.
You) Oh, I like big dogs. (You put a ✓ in your space, and an **x** for partner a)

When you're finished, find another person ("partner b") and get their information.

Verbs past tense and past participle

Word box

worn	drunk	fallen off
found	had	bought
been to	given	seen

Fill in the blanks using words from the word box.

1. Have you ever_____cappuccino?
2. Have you ever_____someone flowers?
3. Have you ever_____your bicycle?
4. Have you ever_____something very expensive?
5. Have you ever_____a World Heritage Site?
6. Have you ever_____a snake?
7. Have you ever_____the flu?*
8. Have you ever_____any money?
9. Have you ever_____a costume?

Now, ask your partner the questions. Partner, answer "Yes, I have" or "No, I haven't".

Next, make your own questions. (You can use the verb list in the back of the book)

1._____?

2._____?

3._____?

Now, ask your partner the questions, and try to get more information.
Use **information words** (what/when/who/where/why, etc.).
Example:
A) Have you ever made a cake?   A) Have you ever won a prize?
B) Yes I have.   B) Yes I have.
A) What kind?   A) When?
B) I made a cheesecake.   B) I won a TV last year, in the postal lottery.

*influenza

What's the difference? Part Two

Notice the difference in the meanings of these words (they are all **verbs**):

say (to) (said [to])- to express in words.

tell (told)- to explain something, or relate a story or a joke.

talk (talked)- the act of speaking or discussing.

Fill in the blanks with the correct words.

At work...

A) You look upset. What's wrong?

B) Yeah, the boss _____ me I have to do overtime tonight. I just called my girlfriend to cancel our date.

A) What did she _____?

B) She _____ me to take a hike...

At the library...

A) Shhhh! No _____ing!

B) Oh, sorry...

At school...

A) Where were you this morning? You missed the exam!

B) Yeah, I know. My alarm didn't go off, and I overslept!

A) What did you _____ the teacher?

B) I _____ her that I was chased by a wild boar and was late for school.

A) What did she _____?

B) She _____ that there are no boars in this area...

With a friend...

A) Vous êtes très jolie!

B) What did you _____?

A) I _____ "You are very pretty" in French.

B) Wow! _____ it again!

Questionnaire-

1. What do you and your friends like to talk about? _____

2. If you won the lottery, would you tell your friends or family? _____

3. Can you say "I love you" in another language? _____

The Conversation Game

Roll the die, read the question, and answer it. Another member in the group will ask you a question.

What did you buy recently, that was a waste of money?	Roll again	What is something you're not very good at doing?	**FINISH**
What is something you need to improve?		What is a sound you really hate?	If you won the lottery, what would you do tomorrow?
What are you really into now?		What is something you need to get rid of?	What can you do really well?
What do you feel like doing now?		What kind of clothes do you like?	What do you want to do during your next vacation?
What is something you've always wanted to do?		Tell about an event you plan to go to soon.	What is something you like to see in the morning?
What is something you **refuse** to eat?		What was the last store you went to? What did you buy?	What smell do you like?
Tell about something you know how to do.		What will you be doing in 10 years?	Roll again (but go BACK!)	What are 5 things you always carry with you?

START

- 51 -

Countries and nationalities

Match the product with the country that produces it.

1. pasta
2. hybrid cars
3. champagne
4. black tea
5. kimchee
6. Hollywood movies
7. bananas
8. coffee
9. caviar
10. beer

a. France
b. The USA
c. Japan
d. Korea
e. Brazil
f. Italy
g. Germany
h. India
i. Ecuador
j. Iran

Now, write sentences like this: (use the word box below for adjectives)
Champagne is produced in France. Champagne is French.

1. _____
2. _____
3. _____
4. _____
5. _____
6. _____
7. _____
8. _____
9. _____

What imported items do you have or use?
Example: *I have a Korean fan. It's from Korea.*
I use a Swiss watch. It's from Switzerland.

_____
_____
_____

What things are produced in *your* country? If you use them, make a ✓.

_____   _____
_____   _____
_____   _____
_____   _____
_____   _____

| French   German   Thai   Ecuadorian   Mexican   Italian   Korean |
| Brazilian   Iranian   Japanese   Chinese   American   English   Australian |
| Indian   Swiss   Spanish   Cambodian   Canadian   Irish   Dutch |

Describing things
Giving details and using adjectives to make a description of a thing or person.

Describe these things. Give details. And *don't* say what the thing is!

1. An animal

Example: It has soft fur. It is gray. It has big claws. It eats plants.

_____
_____
_____

2. One thing you are wearing now.

Example: (teacher, give example of something you are wearing now!)

_____
_____
_____

3. The person sitting next to you.

_____
_____
_____

4. Your *ideal* vacation spot.

_____
_____
_____
_____

Now, have your partner(s) read the description in #4 and decide on a good place for your vacation. _____

Travel Plans

You and your partner are deciding where to go on your next vacation.
Choose one of the destinations below, and fill in the conversation.

A) Where should we go on our next vacation?
B) How about _____, in _____?
A) Sounds great! What can we do there?
B) Well, we can _____ and
_____.
A) How about the food? What's good to eat there?
B) ____(city)____ is famous for _____
and _____.
A) What's _____?
B) It's _____.
A) Sounds excellent! I'll call the travel agency now!

(When you finish, change roles use another destination!)

Now, *you* decide a destination:

Destination: _____
Activities:
• _____
• _____
Good to eat:
• _____
• _____
Explanation of food:
(_____)

A) Where should we go on our next vacation?
B) How about _____, in _____?
A) Sounds great! What can we do there?
B) Well, we can _____ and
_____.
A) How about the food? What's good to eat there?
B) ____(city)____ is famous for _____
and _____.
A) What's _____?
B) It's _____.
A) Sounds excellent! I'll call the travel agency now!

Sydney, Australia
Sights:
- go sightseeing in the city
- take a day trip to Ayers Rock

Good to eat:
- alligator steak
- Tim-tams
  (chocolate-covered cookies)

Siem Reap, Cambodia
Sights:
- visit Angkor Wat
- shop at the Old Market

Good to eat:
- noodle soup
- "amok" (fish or chicken cooked in coconut milk)

Rome, Italy
Sights:
- see the Colosseum
- go to the Vatican City

Good to eat:
- pizza
- "fettucini alfredo"
(pasta in cream sauce)

Honolulu, Hawaii
Sights:
- see Diamondhead
- swim at Waikiki Beach

Good to eat:
- big steaks
- "locomoco" (rice topped with a hamburger patty, a fried egg and gravy)

Homophones *part two*

Read the words, pronounce them and then use them in the conversations.

week	waist	pour	tail	bare	mail	hear
weak	waste	poor	tale	bear	male	here

1. A) Can you _____ me some more coffee?
   B) Sure, pass me your cup.

   C) I had to take my dog to the vet yesterday. He was hit by a car!
   D) Oh, that's terrible! _____ thing!

2. A) Oh no, where are my keys? I think they're lost!
   B) Stop panicking, they're right over _____...

   C) Can you take out the garbage?
   D) What did you say? I can't _____ you.

3. A) My sister just bought a new Italian designer handbag. She said it cost $1000!
   B) $1000 for a handbag?! That's a _____ of money!

   C) What's wrong? Why aren't you wearing your nice, new belt?
   D) I ate too much last week, and it's too tight around my _____ now!

4. A) Did you tell your friends about the party on Friday?
   B) Yeah, I sent all of them _____ this morning.

   C) Help me fill out this passport application. What does this "M/F" mean here?
   D) Oh, you're a boy, so check the "M" box. It means _____.

5. A) Can you see any wild animals in Hokkaido?
   B) Oh, sure, we see foxes all the time, and the occasional _____.

   C) Let's go for a walk on the beach.
   D) I can't walk in my _____ feet, the sand is too hot. Let me get my sandals first!

6. A) I heard you had the H1N1 flu last _____. How are you feeling now?
   D) Oh, I'm much better now, but I still feel a little _____.

7. A) I read a book last week, "The _____ of Momotaro, the Peach Boy".
   B) Oh, that's a classic!

   C) [cat] MEEEEOOOOOOW!
   D) [mother] Johnny, STOP THAT! You should NEVER pull on a cat's _____!

Opposites Board game ⇦⇨

Read the question and answer it. Then, ask the person next to you a question using its opposite (in parentheses).

START

- Who is the tallest person in the room? (shortest)
- What is the best diet food? (worst)
- What is the oldest tourist attraction in your city/prefecture? (newest)
- What is the most expensive hobby you have tried? (cheapest)
- Who in this room has the heaviest bag or purse? (lightest)
- What is the coldest month in your city? (hottest)
- What is the fanciest hotel you have stayed in? (simplest)
- Roll again! ⇦⇨
- What is the most exciting sport you have seen? (most boring)
- What is your favorite wild animal? (tame animal)
- Who in this room is the most studious/hardworking? (laziest)
- Who in your group has the biggest hands? (smallest)
- What sweet foods do you like? (sour)
- Who is the most interesting person on TV? (most boring)
- What is the hardest thing you have ever slept on? (softest)
- What is the scariest animal at the zoo? (friendliest)
- What is the most difficult thing you study/learn? (easiest)
- Who is the strongest person in this room? (weakest)
- Who in this room has the longest hair? (shortest)
- What was your highest cell phone bill? (lowest)
- Who is the loudest person in the room? (quietest)
- Who in this room has the thickest wallet? (thinnest)

FINISH

Usage- when and when not to use "to"

To is used when indicating a specific place, and is **not used** before a verb.

Examples:

I'm going to the bank
She's going to school today.
We went to San Francisco.

They are going to Disneyland next week.
He goes to the supermarket every Sunday.
Do you go to the pool in the summer?

It is not used before a verb. Examples:

I'm going camping.
She's going shopping today.
We went hiking in the mountains.

They are going bird watching next week.
He goes fishing every Sunday.
Do you go swimming in the summer?

Now, fill in the blanks with "go" or "go to" and practice the conversations.

A) Let's _____ shopping tomorrow!
B) OK, where should we go?
A) Why don't we _____ the new mall?
B) Oh, all right, I haven't been there yet.

C) Want to _____ skiing with me next weekend?
D) Sorry, I already have plans to _____ snowboarding with my family.

E) Are you doing anything today?
F) Yeah, I have to _____ the hospital to visit my grandfather.
E) Too bad, I wanted to _____ fishing with you…

G) So, what are your plans for the weekend?
H) I'll probably _____ the amusement park. How about you?
G) Oh, I don't know…I might _____ bowling with some friends…

Where did *you go* recently? (Or what did you do?)
Write 3 sentences using "go" or "go to".

1. _____

2. _____

3. _____

TRIVIA GAME

Culture	Sports	Music	Geography	Food
10	10	10	10	10
20	20	20	20	20
30	30	30	30	30
40	40	40	40	40
50	50	50	50	50

How to play:

Get into groups (5 people or more). One person will be the MC and will read the problems. The other members will form teams (one person will keep score). Team members will take turns selecting a category; "**Sports** for **10 points**" etc, and if the team cannot answer correctly, the other team(s) can answer, or select another category/point value. Have fun!☺

Present perfect tense with *Already & Yet*
(using have+ the past participle to answer questions about things you do)

Examples:

A) Did you wash your car this week?
B) Yes, I've <u>already</u> <u>washed</u> it.

C) Did you take a shower today?
D) Yes, I've <u>already</u> <u>taken</u> one.

E) Did you try that new cake shop?
F) No, I haven't <u>tried</u> it <u>yet</u>.

G) Have you seen your boyfriend today?
H) No, I don't have a boyfriend!

Now, practice asking and answering the questions with your partner.
You decide who is **A** and who is **B**. Make two more questions yourself (#8 & #9)
Write **your answers** on the lines.

Student A:
1. Did you do the laundry this week? _____
2. Did you watch the news today? _____
3. Did you eat dinner yet? _____
4. Did you go grocery shopping this week? _____
5. Did you brush/comb your hair today? _____
6. Did you clean your room? _____
7. Did you call your family? _____
8. _____? _____
9. _____? _____

Student B:
1. Did you wash the dishes today? _____
2. Did you eat breakfast today? _____
3. Did you take out the garbage this week? _____
4. Did you buy some new clothes this season? _____
5. Did you brush your teeth today? _____
6. Did you feed your pet today? _____
7. Did you check your e-mail today? _____
8. _____? _____
9. _____? _____

Extra practice: Talk about your day today...
- I've already_____.
- I've already_____.
- I haven't_____ yet.
- I haven't_____ yet.

Fruit and Vegetable Crossword

Use the fruit & vegetable pages to help you with the spelling!

Across

1. This fruit is used in "sweet and sour pork".
3. This long, green vegetable is used in Italian cooking.
5. It looks like an orange, but is smaller & softer.
8. Ketchup is made from this.
10. You can dig (and eat) this in the spring.
11. This large, stinky fruit is from Southeast Asia.
12. This is a dried plum.
13. The juice from this fruit is used in a cocktail called a "screwdriver".
14. This small, green fruit grows on a tree, and is used to make oil.
16. This leafy vegetable has a lot of iron.

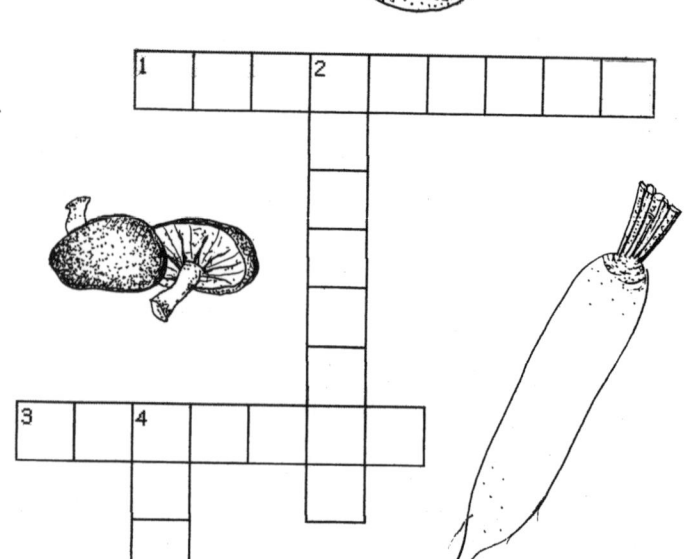

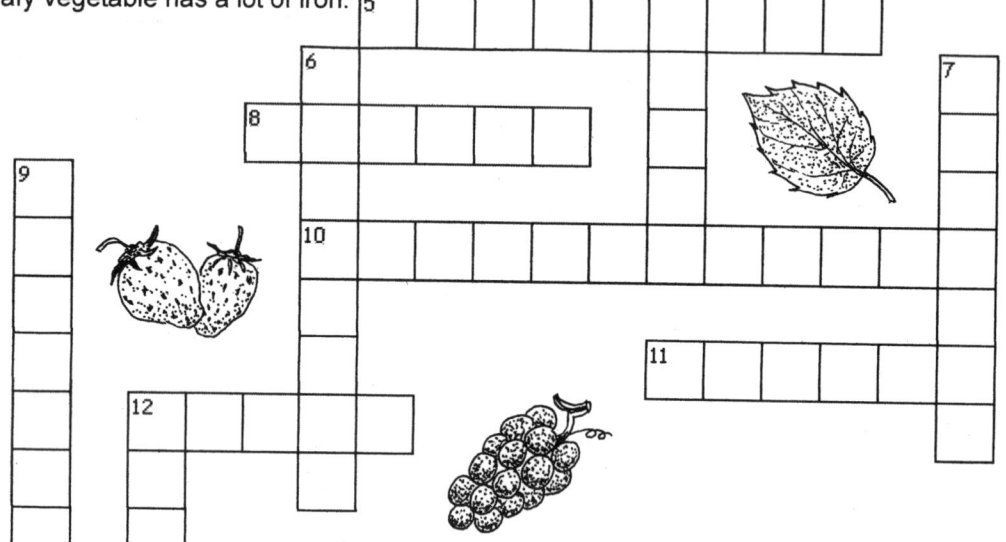

Down

2. This vegetable is purple.
4. The liqueur "Crème de cassis" is made from this fruit.
6. Tofu is made from this.
7. These are dried grapes.
9. This looks like broccoli, only it's white.
12. You use these to make French fries.
15. This is a common Japanese mushroom.

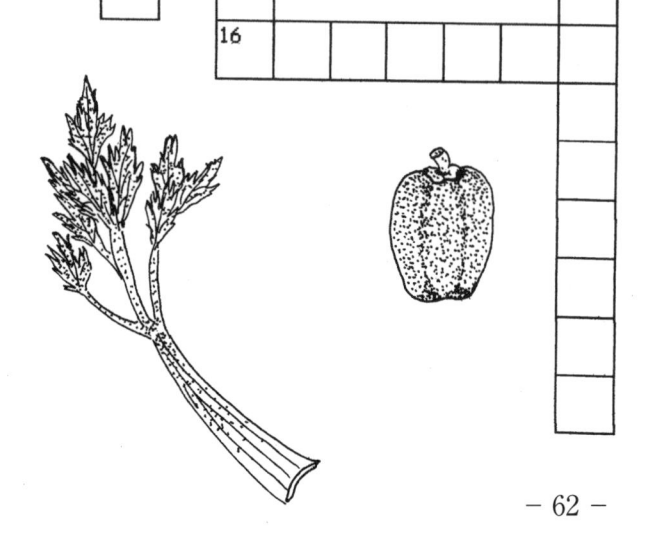

Word usage- *With*
With can be used in many ways. Read the following examples.

I went to the party **with** my friend.   She speaks **with** a French accent.
We usually have soup **with** dinner.   I write **with** a pen.
That scarf is nice **with** that sweater.   My friend is the girl **with** blond hair.

Practice the conversations below.

What do you use to eat it?

A) How do you eat
- noodles
- steak
- a sandwich
- pudding
- pizza
- pasta
- curry

?

- a fork
- a spoon
- a knife and fork
- chopsticks
- my hand

B) With_____.

Who is it?

C) Who's ___(the name of a student)___ ?
D) She's/ He's the one with_____.

- glasses
- long, brown hair
- the strange T-shirt
- the blue dress
- _____

Who did you go with?

E) Where did you go_____?
F) I went to_____.
E) Who did you go with?
F) I went with _____.
   (or "I went by myself.")

- a few months ago
- during the last holiday
- on New Year's Day
- last year
- during the last vacation

How do you like it?

G) I like my _____with _____.
   How about you?
H) I like my _____with _____.
   (or "Me too!")

- tea/coffee
  (cream / sugar / lemon, etc)
- omelet
  (ketchup / salt & pepper, etc)
- grilled fish
  (soy sauce / lemon / tartar sauce, etc)
- hamburger
  (ketchup & mustard / mayonnaise, etc)
- pizza
  (green peppers, onions, salami, etc)
- salad
  (tomatoes / Italian dressing, etc)

Compound words

These are words made up of two different words.
Read the examples:

straw + berry = strawberry   news + paper = newspaper

no + body = nobody   birth + day = birthday

Now, see if you can make compound words. The first are *very easy*.

Novice level

base	grand	bed	play
black	head	cup	in

1. _____ground
2. _____ache
3. _____board
4. _____ball

5. _____father
6. _____cake
7. _____side
8. _____room

Intermediate level

bow	pack	port	ache
stick	fast	stairs	works

1. fire_____
2. break_____
3. back_____
4. air_____

5. rain_____
6. down_____
7. tooth_____
8. lip_____

Genius level

lace	fire	keeper	scare
mill	black	night	cuffs

1. hand_____
2. _____crow
3. _____mare
4. goal_____

5. neck_____
6. _____out
7. wind_____
8. _____place

Can you think of some more compound words? Write them below:

_____   _____   _____   _____

When was the last time you...

Here are some ways to talk about things you have done in the past. Study the expressions in the box below:

(about) 20 seconds ago / 30 minutes ago	Also:
a minute ago	last week
an hour ago / 3 hours ago	last month
a week ago / 6 weeks ago	last February
a month ago / 2 months ago	last year
a year ago / 5 years ago	

Now, read the sample conversation below.

A) When was the last time you made a cake?
B) Oh, about a month ago. How about you?
A) About 10 years ago!

(or *I never make cakes! / I 've never made a cake! / Oh, I can't remember!*)

Student A ask student B: "When was the last time you ..."
(Be sure to add two of your own ideas!)
1. ...had a headache?
2. ...washed your hands?
3. ...ate ice cream?
4. ...saw a rainbow?
5. ...bought some new clothes?
6. ...took a vacation?
7. ...went to a convenience store?
8. ...went to the hospital?
9. ..._____?
10. ..._____?

Student B ask student A:
1. ...saw a movie at a theater?
2. ...rode a bicycle?
3. ...read an interesting book?
4. ...had a cup of tea?
5. ...ate grilled beef?
6. ...tripped and fell down?
7. ...had a cold?
8. ...went swimming?
9. ..._____?
10. ..._____?

Analogies

Read the examples in order to understand the meaning of the word **analogy.** Then, fill in the chart with the best analogies.

Examples: Red is to hot as blue is to cold.

One is to single as two is to double.

1. **teacher** is to **teach** as **student** is to…	
2. **snow** is to **mountain** as **sand** is to…	
3. **eyes** is to **see** as **teeth** is to…	
4. **dog** is to **puppy** as **cat** is to…	
5. **America** is to **president** as **Japan** is to…	
6. **fish** is to **river** as **bird** is to…	
7. **store** is to **shop** as **movie theater** is to…	
8. **writer** is to **book** as **singer** is to…	
9. **coin** is to **metal** as **bill** is to…	
10. **tennis** is to **racket** as **baseball** is to…	
11. **microscope** is to **look** as **microphone** is to…	
12. **boots** is to **winter** as **sandals** is to…	
13. **pencil** is to **lead** as **egg** is to…	

Now, can you make some of your own?

1._____

2._____

3._____

Blood Types What's your blood type?♦
According to fortune-telling by blood type in Japan, this is what your blood type tells you about your character-
(Put a ✓ if you think it is true for you, put an ✗ if you think it's false)

Type A- You have good common sense _____

    You like things to be in order; you are methodical. _____

    You are cooperative and like harmony. _____

    You are careful, you do things with caution. _____

Type B- You think of yourself instead of others. _____

    You are inspirational, have good ideas. _____

    You are easygoing. _____

    You are flexible. _____

Type O- You are realistic. _____

    You don't care much for detail. _____

    You are outgoing; you like being sociable. _____

    You have a good sense of leadership. _____

Type AB- You are an idealist. _____

    You are calm. _____

    You are practical. _____

    You have two different sides. _____

> **Now,** ask 4 people-
> "What's your blood type?"
> _____'s a type ___.
> _____'s a type ___.
> _____'s a type ___.
> _____'s a type ___.

There are also negative words to describe blood types. Here's what they say:

 (Is it true about you? Circle the expressions that are correct!)

"**Type A** is obstinate, and doesn't like change."

"**Type B** only thinks of himself/herself, and doesn't like to work in groups because he/she cannot cooperate well with others."

"**Type O** is careless with details, often acts hastily and is somewhat stubborn."

"**Type AB** often contradicts himself/herself, has strange ideas, and hates people getting in the way."

Blood trivia

♦ In Japan, 40% are type A, 30% are type O, 20% are type B and 10 % are type AB

♦ In the USA, 45% are type O, 40% are type A, 11% are type B and 4% are type AB.

♦ 99% of cats are type A (rarely are they type AB). Dogs have 8 different blood types, characterized by antigens. The most common 2 types are 1-1 and 1-2.

♦ Peruvian Indians are all type O, and Aborigines are either type B or type AB. (No A or O)

Have you ever given blood? If yes, how many times? If not, would you like to try?

_____

How "eco-friendly" are you?
Know these words, and what they mean:

Reduce- to use less of something.
Reuse- to use something more than once.
Recycle- to make an old item into a new, useable item.

What are some things people can reduce (and reduce doing)?
*Hints at bottom of page!!!

_____ _____ _____ _____
_____ _____ _____ _____

What are some things people can reuse?

_____ _____ _____ _____
_____ _____ _____ _____

What are some things people can recycle?

_____ _____ _____ _____
_____ _____ _____ _____

Take this questionnaire with your partner and see who is more "eco-friendly" to the environment.

	me	partner
1. Do you use a composter?	☐	☐
2. Do you use a canvas shopping bag?	☐	☐
3. Do you grow your own fruits / vegetables?	☐	☐
4. Do you (or your family) drive a hybrid car?	☐	☐
5. Do you usually carry a Thermos?	☐	☐
6. Do you ride a bicycle around town?	☐	☐
7. Do you use special LED lights?	☐	☐
8. Do you use bathwater to wash the clothes?	☐	☐
9. Do you mend clothes (instead of throwing them away)?	☐	☐
10. Do you usually bring your own lunch to school/work?	☐	☐

Total: ____ / ____

Ideas for 'reduce, reuse, recycle' section-

styrofoam trays (from fish or meat)   steel cans   aluminum cans   cardboard boxes   bathwater
driving a car   cooking oil   plastic bags   milk cartons   ads from newspapers   glass bottles
batteries   newspapers   plastic(PET) bottles   magazines   old towels & bedsheets

Vocabulary Review Crossword

In this puzzle are words you have (hopefully) learned in this book!

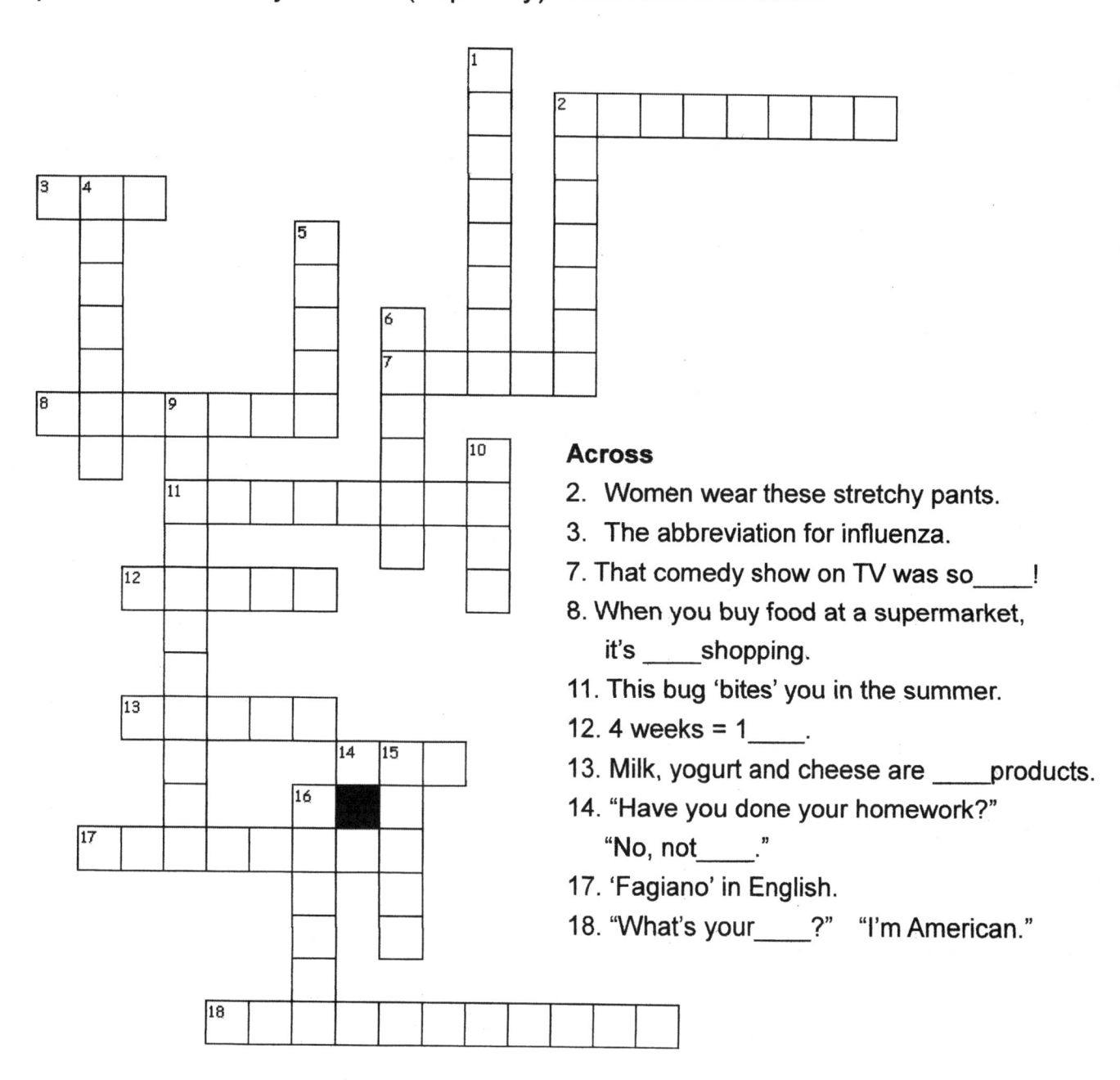

Across
2. Women wear these stretchy pants.
3. The abbreviation for influenza.
7. That comedy show on TV was so____!
8. When you buy food at a supermarket, it's ____shopping.
11. This bug 'bites' you in the summer.
12. 4 weeks = 1____.
13. Milk, yogurt and cheese are ____products.
14. "Have you done your homework?" "No, not____."
17. 'Fagiano' in English.
18. "What's your____?" "I'm American."

Down
1. To say you don't like something is to____.
2. If you buy a ____ticket, you might win some money.
4. Washing clothes is doing the ____.
5. The opposite of 'mild' food is ____food.
6. A lot of people are ____of snakes.
9. These shoes feel nice! They are very ____.
10. It looks like a pig, but it has dark hair, and tusks.
15. I've never ____escargots.
16. You keep your money in it.

- 69 -

Fruit

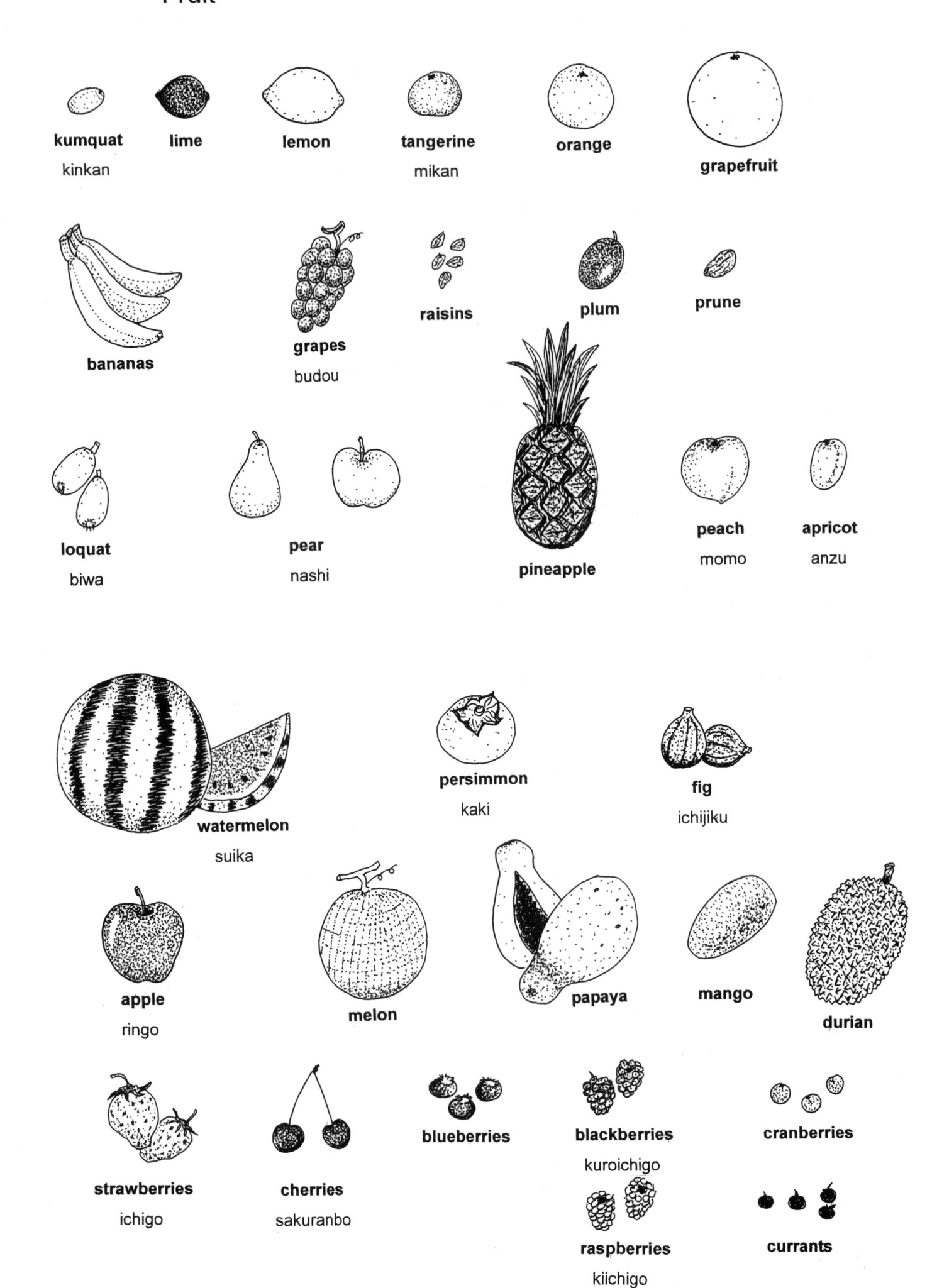

kumquat
kinkan

lime

lemon

tangerine
mikan

orange

grapefruit

bananas

grapes
budou

raisins

plum

prune

loquat
biwa

pear
nashi

pineapple

peach
momo

apricot
anzu

watermelon
suika

persimmon
kaki

fig
ichijiku

apple
ringo

melon

papaya

mango

durian

strawberries
ichigo

cherries
sakuranbo

blueberries

blackberries
kuroichigo

cranberries

raspberries
kiichigo

currants

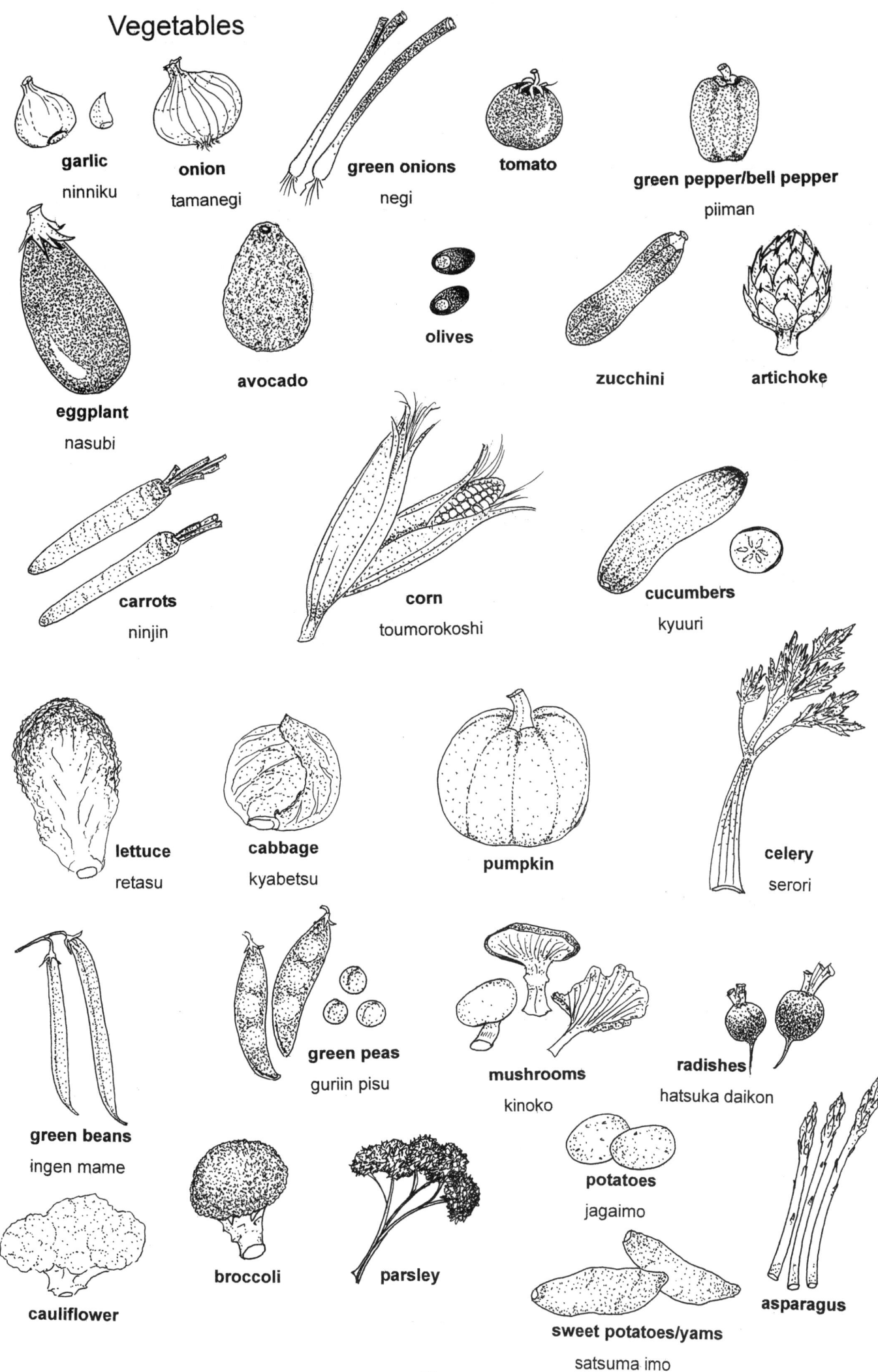

Vegetables

garlic
ninniku

onion
tamanegi

green onions
negi

tomato

green pepper/bell pepper
piiman

eggplant
nasubi

avocado

olives

zucchini

artichoke

carrots
ninjin

corn
toumorokoshi

cucumbers
kyuuri

lettuce
retasu

cabbage
kyabetsu

pumpkin

celery
serori

green peas
guriin pisu

mushrooms
kinoko

radishes
hatsuka daikon

green beans
ingen mame

cauliflower

broccoli

parsley

potatoes
jagaimo

sweet potatoes/yams
satsuma imo

asparagus

- 71 -

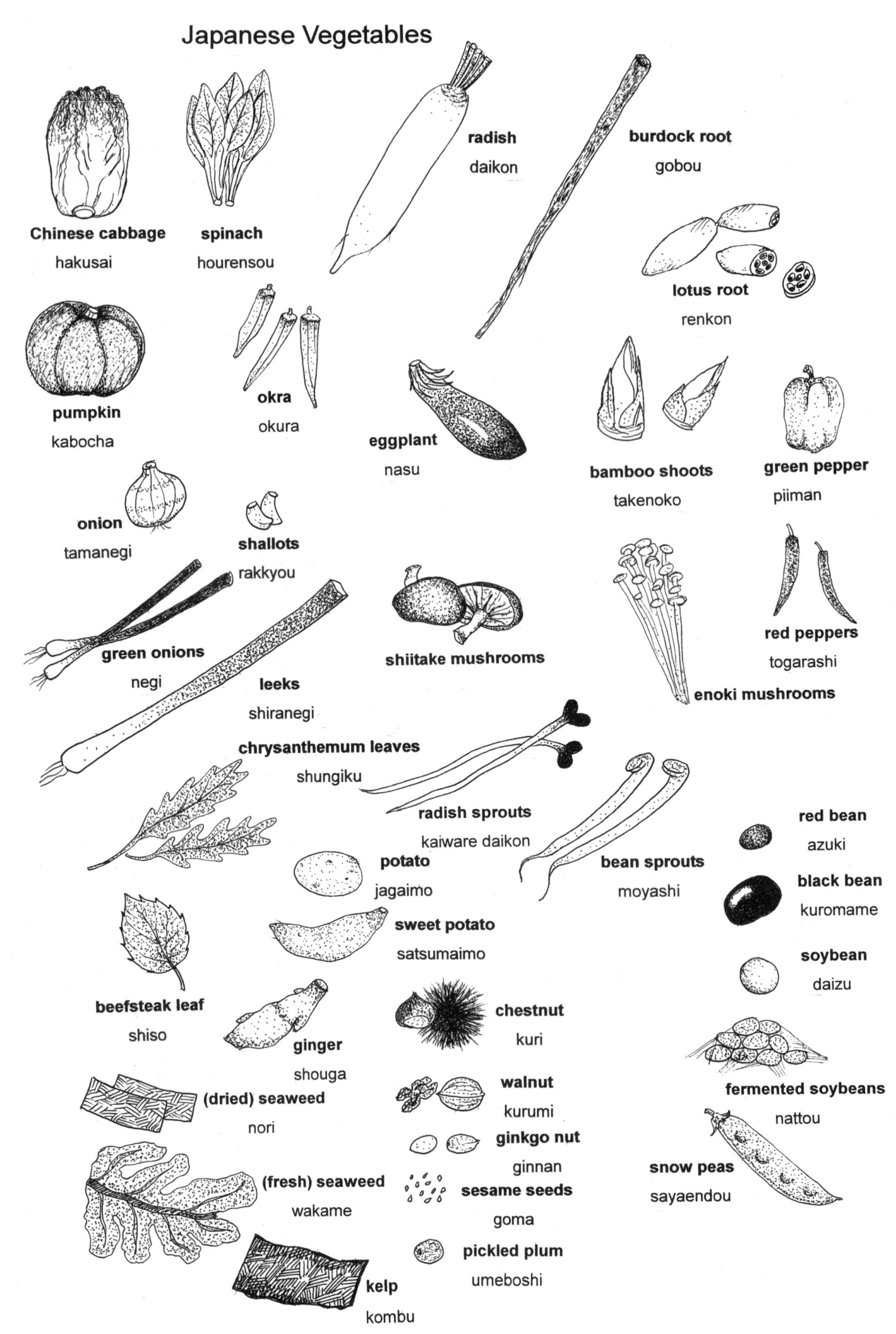

Japanese Vegetables

Chinese cabbage hakusai

spinach hourensou

radish daikon

burdock root gobou

lotus root renkon

pumpkin kabocha

okra okura

eggplant nasu

bamboo shoots takenoko

green pepper piiman

onion tamanegi

shallots rakkyou

shiitake mushrooms

red peppers togarashi

green onions negi

leeks shiranegi

enoki mushrooms

chrysanthemum leaves shungiku

radish sprouts kaiware daikon

bean sprouts moyashi

red bean azuki

potato jagaimo

black bean kuromame

sweet potato satsumaimo

soybean daizu

beefsteak leaf shiso

ginger shouga

chestnut kuri

fermented soybeans nattou

(dried) seaweed nori

walnut kurumi

ginkgo nut ginnan

snow peas sayaendou

(fresh) seaweed wakame

sesame seeds goma

pickled plum umeboshi

kelp kombu

Verb list 動詞表

infinitive/ past tense/ past participle
現在　　　過去　　　過去分詞

be-was/were-been
borrow-borrowed-borrowed
break-broke-broken
bring-brought-brought
buy-bought-bought
catch-caught-caught
come-came-come
cut-cut-cut
do-did-done
drink-drank-drunk
drive-drove-driven
eat-ate-eaten
fall-fell-fallen
find-found-found
fly-flew-flown
forget-forgot-forgotten
get-got-gotten
give-gave-given
go-went-gone
have-had-had
hear-heard-heard
hit-hit-hit
hold-held-held
hurt-hurt-hurt
keep-kept-kept
leave-left-left
lend-lent-lent

lose-lost-lost
make-made-made
meet-met-met
put-put-put
read-read-read
ride-rode-ridden
run-ran-run
say-said-said
see-saw-seen
sell-sold-sold
send-sent-sent
sing-sang-sung
sleep-slept-slept
speak-spoke-spoken
spend-spent-spent
stand-stood-stood
swim-swam-swum
take-took-taken
tear-tore-torn
think-thought-thought
throw-threw-thrown
wake up-woke up-woken up
wear-wore-worn
win-won-won
write-wrote-written

Trivia game questions (for MC only!)

Note: For some of the questions, there are two that you can choose from.
(It's up to you!)

Culture

10 points:
The culture of what part of the world makes totem poles?
(answer: North America)

20 points: Where is reggae music from? (answer: Jamaica)

30 points: If I want to see the statue of King Kamehameha, where do I go?
(answer: Honolulu, Hawaii)

40 points: What meat is not eaten by Muslims? (people who follow the religion of Islam) (answer: pork)

50 points: What is the name of this star? (MC, draw a picture) ✡
(answer: The Star of David) or What religion uses this star? (answer: Jewish)

Sports

10 points: In the USA, soccer is called "soccer". What is the sport called in England? (answer: football)

20 points: In sport, this expression means something that is done 3 times, successfully, in a game. (answer: hat trick)

30 points: What do the letters MVP mean? (answer: most valuable player)

40 points: Where did the sport "curling" originate?
(answer: Scotland or Canada)

50 points: In baseball, you hit the ball with a "bat". In the game of cricket, what do you use to hit the ball? (answer: a "bat")

Music

10 points: What is the name of the most famous violin maker?
(answer: Stradivarius)

20 points: How old was Mozart when he died? (answer: 35 years old)
or What were the white keys of a piano originally made from? (answer: ivory)

30 points: How many strings does a violin have? (answer: four)

40 points: What is "gospel music"? (answer: music that is sung in church)

50 points: How many keys does a piano have? (answer: eighty-eight)
or What does the Italian expression "a cappella" mean?
(answer: "chapel style")

Geography

10 points: This country is famous for its dairy products and tulips.
(answer: the Netherlands / Holland)
20 points: What are the 2 official languages spoken in Canada?
(answer: English and French)
or Where is Mt Everest? (answer: Nepal / Tibet)
30 points: Where did the Olympic Games begin? (What country?)
(answer: Greece)
40 points: This country has many historical attractions, one of them is the city that was buried by volcano ashes. (answer: Italy)
50 points: What are the 2 westernmost states in the US?
(answer: Hawaii and Alaska)

Food

10 points: Where can I eat "locomoco"? (answer: in Hawaii)
or What does "café au lait" mean? (answer: coffee with milk)
20 points: What is "pasta"? (answer: noodles / a paste to make dough for noodles)
30 points: What is "fois gras"? (answer: fatty duck liver)
or What kind of soft bread can I find in India? (answer: "nan")
40 points: In "bird's nest soup", what is the bird's nest made of?
(answer: bird [swallow] saliva)
50 points: What country produces the delicious Godiva chocolate?
(answer: Belgium)

Answer Key

Reading large numbers- Part One (key to match exercise)

1. h   2. e   3. i   4. g   5. a   6. j   7. d   8. c   9. f   10. b

Abbreviations (key to abbreviations in illustrations)

SARS- Severe Acute Respiratory Syndrome
BSE- Bovine Spongiform Encephalopathy
AD- assistant director
DA- District Attorney
PM- private message
ASAP- as soon as possible
AED- Automated External Defibrillator
CPR- Cardiopulmonary resuscitation
PET- Polyethylene terephthalate

Fruit and Vegetable Crossword key

1. pineapple
3. zuccini
5. tangerine
8. tomato
10. bamboo shoots
11. durian
12. prune
13. orange
14. olive
16. spinach

2. eggplant
4. currants
6. soybeans
7. raisins
9. cauliflower
12. potatoes
15. shiitake

Vocabulary Review Crossword key

2. leggings
3. flu
7. funny
8. grocery
11. mosquito
12. month
13. dairy
14. yet
17. pheasant
18. nationality

1. complain
2. lottery
4. laundry
5. spicy
6. afraid
9. comfortable
10. boar
15. eaten
16. wallet

Category

English-Japanese glossary

Acorn-どんぐり
Acrylic-アクリル
Afford-(金の)余裕がある
Afraid-怖がる、怖い
Ailment-病気、問題
Alarm-(~clock) 目覚まし時計
Amusement park-遊園地
Ankle-足首
Antibiotics-抗生物質
Antigens-アンチゲン、抗原
Appliance-電気製品、電気器具
Awful-ひどい、まずい
Baking-お菓子作り
Bare-裸（足・手）
Boar-猪
Born-生まれました
Blood type-血液型
Calm-冷静
Cardiologist-心臓外科
Careful-気をつける、慎重
Category-部門、部類
Caution-注意
Centipede-ムカデ
Certainly-かしこまりました
Cicada-セミ
Cockroach-ゴキブリ
Comfortable-心地よい、楽な
Common-よくあるの
Common sense- 常識
Compress-湿布
Condominium-マンション
Contradict-反する
Cooperative-協調性
Cotton-綿
Crab-かに
Date-日付
Dairy product-乳製品
Definitely-絶対に
Dentist-歯医者
Destination-行き先、目的地
Detail-細かい

Diabetes-糖尿病
Diarrhea-下痢
Difference-違い
Dizzy-めまい
Dragonfly-トンボ
Ear plugs-耳栓
Earthquake-地震
Easygoing-楽天的
ENT-耳鼻科
Eraser-消しゴム
Esophagus-食道
Explanation-説明
Farm-牧場
Fear-恐怖
Female-♀
Field trip-遠足
Flashlight-懐中電灯
Flexible-柔軟な考え
Flour-小麦粉
Folding umbrella-折りたたみ傘
Fortune-telling-占い
Garbage can-ごみ箱
Gargle-うがい
Global warming-地球温暖化
Go off-(alarm)　鳴る
Grocery(~ies)-食料品
Gynecologist-産婦人科
Handstand-逆立ち
Hay fever-花粉症
Hot spring-温泉
Ideal-理想的な
Idealist-理想追求型
Imported-輸入品
Inspirational-ひらめき
Jellyfish-クラゲ
Language-言葉
Laundry-洗濯
Leadership-親分肌
Leather-皮、牛革
Light bulb-電灯
Lightning-稲妻
Linen-麻

Lottery-くじ、宝くじ	Runny nose-鼻水（が出る）
Lovely-きれい、かわいい	Saw-鋸
Male-♂	Scar-傷跡
Medicine-薬	Sink- 流し台、洗面所
Methodical-几帳面	Snail-カタツムリ
Microscope-顕微鏡	Sociable-社交的
Mosquito-蚊	Sore throat-のどが痛い
Nap-昼寝	Spell-綴り、綴る
Nationality-国籍・〜籍	Sprain-ねんざ
Nauseous-吐き気（がある）	Spend-(お金)がかかる、(時間)を過ごす
Nutritionist-栄養士	
Obesity-肥満	Stadium-スタジアム
Obstinate-頑固	Stapler-ホッチキス
Ophthalmologist-眼科	Starving-とてもおなかがすいた
Osteoporosis-骨粗鬆症	Stethoscope-聴診器
Otorhinolaryngology-耳鼻科	Stiff shoulders-肩こる、肩こり
Outgoing-外向的	Stubborn-頑固
Overtime-残業	Suburbs-郊外
Pediatrician-小児科	Sunscreen-日焼け止め
Perfume-香水	Superlative-最上級
Pharmacist-薬剤師	Thermometer-体温計、温度計
Pheasant-きじ	Tale-物語
Platinum-プラチナ	Taste-趣味、好み
Plural-複数形	Thunder-雷
Pomegranate-ザクロ	Titanium-チタン
Poor-可哀想な	Torn-(down)-壊しました
Popular-人気	Trip-躓く
Populated-人込み	Two-story (house)-二階建て
Pour-注ぐ	Unusual-珍しい、変わっている
Practical-合理的	Urologist-泌尿器科
Probably-かもしれない	Useful-役に立つ
Produce(d)-製作する	Vinyl-ビニール
Product-商品	Volcano-火山
Pronounce-発音をする	Vote-投票する
Puppy-子犬	Waste-無駄使い
Questionnaire-アンケート	Wallet-財布
Radiologist-放射線技術家	Weather-天気
Raw-生	Whistle-口笛
Realistic-現実的	Wrap-巻く
Refrigerator-冷蔵庫	World Heritage Site-世界遺産
Restroom-お手洗い	
Rice cooker-炊飯器	

■著者紹介

Karen A. Stafford（カレン・スタフォード）

米国・カルフォルニア出身、1985年来日。
現在、英会話教室と岡山県内の4大学で教えています。

テキストシリーズ

Modern English for Conversation（大学教育出版、2008年）
Still more... Modern English for Conversation（大学教育出版、2010年）

More...
Modern English for Conversation

2010年4月10日　初版第1刷発行
2014年4月25日　初版第2刷発行
2017年4月25日　初版第3刷発行
2023年3月20日　初版第4刷発行

■著　　者──── Karen A. Stafford
■発 行 者──── 佐藤　守
■発 行 所──── 株式会社 大学教育出版
　　　　　　　　〒700-0953　岡山市南区西市855-4
　　　　　　　　　　電話 (086)244-1268(代)　FAX (086)246-0294
■印刷製本──── サンコー印刷㈱
■装　　丁──── ティーボーンデザイン事務所

Ⓒ Karen A. Stafford 2010, Printed in Japan
検印省略　　落丁・乱丁本はお取り替えいたします。
無断で本書の一部または全部を複写・複製することは禁じられています。

ISBN978−4−88730−973−9